"*Fresh Produce Shipping* provides a 'go to guide' for Importers/Exporters, Loss adjusters, Fresh Produce Surveyors, students with an interest in Fresh Produce shipping and claims handling, by providing a comprehensive realistic understanding of the market in an easy to understand text. The book provides a step by step understanding of the claims handling process covering both Airline and Ocean shipments providing reference guides and an understanding of the various conventions relevant to both forms of shipping."

– **Victoria Bredin**, *British Association of Cargo Surveyors*

FRESH PRODUCE SHIPPING

This book is an in-depth study of air and ocean goods-in-transit claims. It sets out to guide and assist businesses within the fresh produce industry to successfully implement the best processes and procedures to maximise their recovery efforts against contracted carriers.

Fresh Produce Shipping focuses heavily on protecting the rights and recovery aspects of companies involved in growing, selling, and transporting fresh produce. It gives importers, exporters, loss adjusters, surveyors, and freight forwarders an easy-to-understand guide to the management and requirements of submitting claims. It provides an overview of the shipping terms and procedures involved when raising a claim. The book offers specific and detailed industry knowledge to stakeholders who would not normally have access to such information without the employment of specialists or legal counsel, providing an inexperienced reader with the tools to submit a claim and achieve a sufficient understanding of the procedures involved.

A valuable guide and comprehensive reference for parties seeking compensation for lost or damaged goods, this book will be of relevance to shippers and importers of fresh produce, lawyers acting for commercial clients and underwriters, cargo surveyors, trade bodies around the world representing fresh produce operators, and forwarders wishing to support their clients.

Rex C. Tester spent two years with Pan Am as an aircraft loader from 1969 and transferred to the Cargo Division in 1971. For the next three years he worked in Cargo Operations and became a certified loadmaster. In 1974, he was entrusted with Pan Am's European cargo claims. In 1983, he became independent, and has worked on all aspects of ocean and air cargo claims, including surveying and investigations at all levels.

MARITIME AND TRANSPORT LAW LIBRARY

Ship Building, Sale and Finance
Edited by Bariş Soyer and Andrew Tettenborn

The Modern Law of Marine Insurance
Volume 4
Edited by D. Rhidian Thomas

Air Cargo Insurance
Malcom A. Clarke and George Leloudas

Offshore Oil and Gas Installations Security
An International Perspective
Mikhail Kashubsky

International Trade and Carriage of Goods
Edited by Bariş Soyer and Andrew Tettenborn

Maritime Law and Practice in China
Liang Zhao and Lianjun Li

Maritime Cross-Border Insolvency
Lia Athanassiou

The Law of Yachts and Yachting
Second Edition
Edited by Filippo Lorenzon and Richard Coles

Maritime Liabilities in a Global and Regional Context
Edited by Bariş Soyer and Andrew Tettenborn

New Technologies, Artificial Intelligence and Shipping Law in the 21st Century
Edited by Bariş Soyer and Andrew Tettenborn

The Law of Wreck
Nicholas Gaskell and Craig Forrest

Codification of Maritime Law
Challenges, Possibilities and Experience
Edited by Zuzanna Pepłowska-Dąbrowska and Justyna Nawrot

Transport Documents in Carriage Of Goods by Sea
International Law and Practice
By Caslav Pejovic

Maritime Law
Fifth Edition
Edited by Yvonne Baatz

Ship Operations: New Risks, Liabilities and Technologies in the Maritime Sector
Edited by Bariş Soyer and Andrew Tettenborn

Maritime Safety in Europe
Edited by Justyna Nawrot and Zuzanna Pepłowska-Dąbrowska

Fresh Produce Shipping
Damages and Compensation
Rex C. Tester

FRESH PRODUCE SHIPPING

DAMAGES AND COMPENSATION

REX C. TESTER

informa law
from Routledge

First published 2022
by Routledge
2 Park Square, Milton Park, Abingdon, Oxon OX14 4RN

and by Routledge
605 Third Avenue, New York, NY 10158

Routledge is an imprint of the Taylor & Francis Group, an Informa business

British Library Cataloguing-in-Publication Data
A catalogue record for this book is available from the British Library

Library of Congress Cataloguing-in-Publication Data
Names: Tester, Rex C., author.
Title: Fresh produce shipping: damages and compensation / Rex C. Tester.
Description: Abingdon, Oxon; New York, NY: Routledge, 2022. |
Series: Maritime and transport law library | Includes bibliographical references and index.
Identifiers: LCCN 2021023623 (print) | LCCN 2021023624 (ebook) |
ISBN 9781032112848 (hardback) | ISBN 9781003219231 (ebook)
Subjects: LCSH: Freight insurance–Law and legislation–Great Britain. |
Freight insurance–Law and legislation. |
Farm produce–Transportation–Law and legislation–Great Britain. |
Farm produce–Transportation–Law and legislation. | Insurance claims–Great Britain.
Classification: LCC KD1887.F74 T47 2022 (print) | LCC KD1887.F74 (ebook) |
DDC 343.09/32–dc23
LC record available at https://lccn.loc.gov/2021023623
LC ebook record available at https://lccn.loc.gov/2021023624

ISBN: 9781032112848 (hbk)
ISBN: 9781032112862 (pbk)
ISBN: 9781003219231 (ebk)

DOI: 10.4324/9781003219231

Typeset in Times New Roman
by Deanta Global Publishing Services, Chennai, India

Dedicated to the lovely Jenny and to the revered memory of Helen – the two spectacular ladies who recklessly linked their lives to mine – for their encouragement;

In passing, and with thanks, Margaret, whose chance remark long, long ago unknowingly launched me on my career; and,

Finally, to Jenna and Lee, whom I am proud to call my daughter and son.

CONTENTS

ACKNOWLEDGEMENTS

Firstly, a giant thank you to Andrew Bicknell, of Clyde & Co., for his guidance and support over several years in marine matters, and, who – it seems – remains on good terms with me, despite ploughing through this book to put me right on points and interpretation of law, and to correct my editing!

David Reynolds, also of Clyde & Co., with his varying teams over many years, for his guidance and support in my work. Also, a member of his team, Sean Marriott, for his significant contribution in respect of quantum and other issues.

Stuart Armstrong, of Hill Dickinson, for his guidance and support in aviation matters over many years.

Bertrand Courtois and Victoire Revenaz of Lexline in Paris, for their guidance and support in marine matters in France.

Markus Hauser, of Blaum, Dettmer, Rabstein in Bremen, for his guidance and support in marine matters in Germany.

I cannot overlook my clients, past and present, who have placed their trust in me for so many years: Leena Malde of Wealmoor, James Bartington of Flamingo Fresh Produce, and Christopher Sims of J. O. Sims, and there are numerous others in Continental Europe, South America, India, Ireland, and Egypt.

Finally, there are Network Airline Services, and, my great friend, Brian Lawrence, of Westgate Handling Services who have from time to time instructed me on 'interesting' cases, for which a great deal of head-scratching has resulted in solutions for them.

All my clients have provided me with stimulating, and at times, immensely frustrating challenges to succeed on their behalves.

FOREWORD

In 1974, I was thrust into a job within Pan American World Airways which I did not want: the airline was undergoing one of its periodic contractions (irreversible, as it turned out) and I was in no position to argue about my manager's decision.

It took around six months for me to develop any enthusiasm in the work, and it arose from what I perceived to be an almost total lack of knowledge outside of Pan Am HQ of the disciplines involved in handling 'cargo claims'. It seems that no-one within the company could or would guide me, and HQ did not seem willing to give me any help – they just handed down edicts, it seemed.

I burned to learn how to do my job. A friendly solicitor – well known and highly respected in aviation circles now – gave me a 'kick-start'.

My first attempt at publication was a little disappointing. I eventually wrote a Cargo Claims Handling Manual for Pan Am and submitted it to HQ for consideration. I received no acknowledgement, only to see it distributed throughout Pan Am some months later largely unchanged and with no credit accorded me!

Nonetheless, I did enjoy my job, which seemed to evolve into a vocation, but also it was responsible in 1983, against all apparently sane advice, for my becoming independent, and commencing a business life of great variety, not a few scares, and, overall, tremendous satisfaction.

My experience – I believe – has been unique: neither loss adjuster nor surveyor in the traditional mould, nor lawyer, I developed my technical legal knowledge and combined it with practical operational knowledge. I seemed to be in a unique position to carry out Surveys and Investigations for Insurers and Commercial Clients and unbound by traditional practices I worked on some major international losses, once or twice even courting physical danger in West Africa!

From my present viewpoint, it seems to have been inevitable that my sense of pragmatism would become highly developed: constantly searching for the truly practical way forward – without ignoring moral considerations; and operating on principle only when I was sure the client understood truly the position he was taking (and for which he was ultimately paying).

As time went on, in the early 1990s, I was asked by clients to undertake claims against ocean carriers, a very different situation to dealing with air carriers, and this was at a time when my work became more and more concerned with fresh produce shipping generally.

In 1998, I wrote *Air Cargo Claims* – part of the series of 'Aviation Practical Guides' – it sold well…

As time has gone on, and I have become ever more involved in ocean cargo claims for perishable produce from many parts of the world, it has become clear to me, as I approach inevitable retirement, that I should make available to the commercial sector represented by my clients, my experience and knowledge, that they may benefit when I become inactive in this field.

As with my book on *Air Cargo Claims*, this is not intended to be a 'learned' work in the traditional legal sense, and few legal decisions are referred to in detail. Its thrust is one of practicality, distilled from a career of finding practical solutions, since nothing else would suffice.

TABLE OF CASES

DEFINITIONS

Claim value	Quantum.
Datalogger:	Properly applied to the thermograph permanently installed in an ocean reefer container, but sometimes mis-applied to the portable instruments placed in consignments by shippers.
Grower and Shipper:	It should be noted that in many instances in this work, these terms are interchangeable.
Importer and Consignee:	In most cases these are the same entity.
Jurisdiction:	The country or state where the dispute is to be determined legally.
Load list:	Same as packing list but more usually used in an ocean carriage context.
Loss:	Dependent on the context, this will cover actual loss, damage, and delay on the premise that all three create monetary loss.
Multiples:	Supermarkets.
Prima facie:	This is normally written herein as *prima facie*. In legal practice it refers to two things; firstly, that upon initial examination, sufficient corroborative evidence appears to exist to support a case; and, secondly, in common law jurisdictions, *prima facie* denotes evidence that, unless rebutted, would be sufficient to prove a particular proposition or fact.
Packing list:	Same as load list.
Quantum:	Claim value.
Respondent:	This term designates any party which is required to respond, but in general terms in this work, will correspond to the carrier to whom a claim has been submitted.
Shipper and Grower:	It should be noted that in many instances in this work, these terms are interchangeable.
Special Drawing Rights:	(SDRs) The SDR is an international reserve asset (effectively an artificial currency). Its value varies according to a 'basket' of five currencies and can be checked on a daily basis through the internet.
Supermarkets:	Multiples.
Temperature Abuse:	This term defines a situation when a consignment out-turns at destination in a condition indicating that it has been damaged through being allowed to become heated, chilled, or frozen whilst in transit.

Temperature instruments:	The term 'thermograph' is used exclusively to indicate the recording instrument and 'thermogram' to denote the chart produced from the data downloaded from it.
Thermogram:	A chart produced from data downloaded from a thermograph.
Thermograph:	A temperature recording instrument.
Web-track:	Transit histories extracted from airlines' and ocean carriers' websites.

INTRODUCTION

0.1 There can be no doubt that the 'world' of goods-in-transit claims is vastly complicated, and one sector of commerce's experience of this world will differ significantly from another.

0.2 Hence, this book is intended for the benefit of exporters and importers of fresh fruits, vegetables, and flowers moving their consignments by air and by ocean reefer container primarily to the United Kingdom, Northern Europe, and Scandinavia, many of whom appear to be uninsured for transit.

0.3 Undoubtedly, however, much of this book will still be relevant to exporters and importers operating elsewhere.

0.4 Additionally, underwriters, maritime lawyers, cargo surveyors, loss adjusters, and members of the freight industry will be able to derive benefit from it. Even carriers themselves will derive benefit from it.

0.5 Reference to Court cases underlying the principles expounded herein will necessarily and broadly refer to the English Court, but many of those general principles are in force elsewhere in one form or another.

0.6 The primary benefit which can be obtained from this work is to guide claimants in the preparation of sound well-constructed claims in their dealings with carriers; and, in the event that legal action is required, to present those 'well-constructed' cases to their legal representatives enabling them to promptly and efficiently pursue carriers with as little delay as possible.

0.7 Hence, herein there will be some references to applicable law, both arising from international treaties enshrined in statute law and from legal precedent set in various cases brought before the Courts; it is not intended for readers to become expert in such matters, but to obtain a general idea of how and why claims are regulated by such law.

0.8 This work deals with the clear majority of 'straightforward' claims; it does not cover claims where there are unusual situations, or obscure or complex legal arguments are offered in defence by carriers, since, in such cases, expert legal advice should, of course, be sought.

0.9 So, to begin at the beginning, you have a contract to export and supply fruit, vegetables, or flowers to a customer overseas; or you are that importer-customer.

0.10 It is hard work but together you make it work and work well.

0.11 All is well for a while, and then suddenly your ocean container or your air consignment is lost or delivered with the products damaged in some way.

0.12 It could be that when you put the contract together neither of you gave thought to the losses which might happen during transit, and their effects.

0.13 If you are the exporter-supplier you need to be paid for your products, but you know that your customer cannot sell them.

0.14 If you are the importer-buyer you now have nothing to fulfil your supply commitments to the supermarkets or other clients who are expecting it, but you know that your client will brook no excuses for lack of product – and you might even be 'fined' by your customer for failing to fulfil your supply contract.

0.15 Total disruption ensues; perhaps you, as the exporter-supplier, will demand payment, and you as the importer-customer will be unable to make payment. Maybe the relationship breaks down completely and that lucrative contract evaporates, and you go your separate ways to try the same thing with other partners, chastened by experience but not really knowing how to resolve matters if the same thing happens again.

0.16 Familiarity with INCOTERMS and the concepts or risk and title, would have been prudent, but even so, this would not necessarily have resolved the issues between you. Enforcing action under those terms might well have added to the damaging "fall-out".

0.17 Or, as seems to the writer more common, the two of you may agree to work together on getting compensation. You make some kind of agreement in regard to payment for the products – perhaps a part-payment – and agree to 'settle up' when the claim against the carrier has been settled.

0.18 But how – the devil – do you get the carrier to agree to settle?

0.19 There can be no doubt that this is an enigma; the problem is simply based on natural unwillingness to pay a debt if it can be avoided, whether that debt is a trading debt, or a debt of liability.

0.20 Trading debts are not easy to avoid and normally only remain unpaid if the debtor is failing; debts of liability can be fought and the ways in which the parties at fault can avoid them are legion.

0.21 In many situations, it may seem that the dice are loaded against the claimant.

0.22 Every commercial operation must make a profit, and if expenses can be avoided then the end – it seems – can justify the means; in my experience there are honourable carriers, but, sometimes, it is tempting to wonder if these 'opponents' are cynically and deliberately putting every possible obstacle – fair or foul – in the way of claimants.

0.23 However, it is but fair to admit the existence of cynical and dishonest claimants, but fortunately, the writer has encountered less than a handful over a long career.

0.24 This book is devoted to the search for the ways to obtain compensation for your losses.

CHAPTER 1

An overview of the claims process

The loss

1.1 The vast majority of losses suffered on perishable consignments arise through damage from exposure to adverse conditions during transit. Claims arising for consignments actually lost in transit are far fewer and far more straightforward to administer, but these are dealt with in detail below.

1.2 Most of the time you will discover there is a loss when your consignment is collected from the airport and has arrived back at your pack house in a damaged condition.

1.3 Alternatively, your ocean container arrives at your pack-house and on opening it, your quality control staff notice a smell, or probe or sense a warmer-than-expected temperature.

1.4 Maybe you saw that the container vent was closed on arrival, or upon opening you smelt that alcoholic smell which portends major problems.

1.5 Alternatively, the container is de-vanned, and the container is allowed to depart, following which your quality control staff open boxes and find the produce has a problem – perhaps condensation, over-maturity, rots, and so on.

1.6 Maybe you can sort and repack, but it still proves a serious reverse for you. Perhaps you cannot begin to repack for your customer or distribute it because it is simply not good enough.

1.7 Now you have to deal both with the shortfall of product so far as your customer is concerned and decide what to do to get moving with the claim for loss against the defaulting party.

1.8 If you have sufficient throughput you may be able to cover the shortage, but if not, you may have to source it elsewhere and pay a premium for doing so.

1.9 What else can you do?

1.10 Your supermarket customers are not going to be sympathetic unless it is a major problem such as the time in the early 2000s when in excess of 50 containers of melons were offloaded and left in Jamaica, and even the multiples had to accept that this event fell well outside the realm of isolated hiccoughs that an individual importer would be expected to remedy.

1.11 Dealing with the shortage itself falls outside the purview of this book, but the writer is aware of the enormous efforts which you may have to make in this pursuit.

1.12 So, where do you start to tackle your claims problem?

1.13 You cannot start too early: in both air and ocean cargo situations, the immediate priority is to notify the carrier of the problem, but the carriers' reactions are varied and

DOI: 10.4324/9781003219231-1

sometimes surprising, even on isolated occasions, verging on the unreasonable and hostile, making it difficult to believe that you are actually the customer[1] of the carrier.

Air

1.14 On rare occasions, your driver may have detected a problem when collecting from the airport.

1.15 However, there is often significant resistance by the airline's warehousemen to allow your driver to give a claused signature, and your driver knows he cannot protest without the possibility of being subjected to significant aggravation and threats of being offloaded back into the warehouse when he is under orders to get the consignment back to your pack-house as quickly as he can.

1.16 There are numerous anecdotal stories of physical threats to drivers protesting too strongly, and since your driver knows he will have to return for subsequent collections, it is not in his (and, hence, your) interest for him to pursue his discontent too strongly.

1.17 The immediate and most important task is for you to send a notice of claim to the airline with the absolute minimum delay: you must provide reasonable details to enable them to identify the consignment and be aware of the type of damage involved.

1.18 You may call up the airline's cargo office advising of the damage, and you will almost invariably be told to simply send in a claim notice, because much of the time you will not be able to speak to anyone who has expertise in the field of claims.

1.19 It is vital that you extend an invitation to the airline to inspect the cargo for itself; it is highly unlikely to take the opportunity to do so but having declined or ignored the invitation means that they are not in a strong position to challenge your own surveyor's report, and/or your quality control inspection records.

1.20 You are then 'at your ease' – relatively speaking – to gather your evidence of the damage, consider what has caused it, calculate your losses, and prepare and submit the claim to the airline.

1.21 In all but the smallest of losses, it is prudent to immediately instruct an independent surveyor to inspect the damage and produce a report – you will have to pay for this, but you can add the cost to your claim, irrespective of whether the airline disputes that you are entitled to do so.

1.22 Whilst the airline will seldom, if ever, instruct its own surveyor you can be sure that the airline's claims department expects you to produce the survey report as evidence, but despite being given the opportunity to carry out its own survey, it should be no surprise when it disputes the conclusions of your surveyor, despite having not carried out its own.

1.23 Should the matter progress so far as Court, the airline and its advisors will actually know that such challenges are unlikely to be successful unless they can point to a clear and obvious fault in the claimant's survey report.

1 A little thought shows that a consignee, importer, claimant is effectively also the customer of the carrier, despite the shipper having been the party to conclude the contract of carriage. It is quite common for the consignee to stipulate which carriers the shippers should use, and which to avoid.

1.24 Additionally, it has become more difficult for an airline (or ocean carrier, for that matter) to take this line as a result of a case brought in the English Court.[2] However, this is unlikely to stop carriers attempting to dispute the conclusions in a claimant's survey report.

Ocean

1.25 If the container is opened and the problem is immediately obvious, the best thing you can do is close it up, call the carrier, and tell them what has happened and ask them what they would like to do about it.

1.26 Their reaction will normally be that they will instruct a surveyor to inspect the cargo in haste, which must be matched by your instructing a surveyor to act on your behalf.

1.27 The ideal is for the two surveyors to inspect together, so that disputes about the actuality of the damage can be avoided – one hopes also that they can agree on the cause of the damage. However, a joint survey is not always possible.

1.28 If the container can be held until the surveyor or surveyors attend and check it, this will be beneficial since it is possible that the cause of the damage will be promptly discovered as a result of inspection of it and its settings.

1.29 More often it is the case that surveyors are not immediately available, and as a consequence the container cannot be held at your pack-.0house.

1.30 Following departure of the unloaded container from your pack-house, be aware that you cannot expect the carrier to check it out and report back to you as regards any problem – they will be reluctant to disclose that evidence, and only litigation or a credible threat of it will force out the details of whatever inspection they may have done.

The strategy to be adopted

1.31 There can be no alternative to 'front loading' your actions in regard to any claim; find the time to do the claim preparation work right at the beginning.

1.32 As aforementioned, the prerequisite need is to put the carrier on immediate notice and be as certain as possible that they have received that notice. You can reasonably depend on ocean carriers to respond, but air carriers' responses are less certain, and they will range from reasonable responses to apparently being completely ignored.

1.33 Then, if you can gather your evidence while it is 'fresh', much heartache can be avoided at a later stage, when the carrier or its solicitor perhaps demands to see something which may need extended searching of your archives – if it has not been dumped in the interim.

1.34 Alternatively, as an importer, trying to get pre-shipment evidence from your supplier will always be problematical if not done at the outset; and consider how you will deal with a situation where you no longer take product from that supplier.

1.35 Thus, place all emphasis on gathering all relevant papers.

1.36 Gather transit documents, quality control reports, the surveyor's report, pre-shipment evidence, and a clear understanding as far as possible of the transit history together

2 Griffiths -v- TUI UK Limited [2020] EWHC 2268 (QB).

with – in the case of air carriage – weather reports at origin, transhipment points, and destination if there is temperature abuse as so often happens, so that you can point to a probability of your consignment having been left out in ambient temperatures.

1.37 Many a case has been lost because the claimant was required to prove the consignment was in sound condition and at the right temperature when loaded into the container or delivered to the airline, and a year to two after the loss, it has proved impossible to locate that proof.

1.38 A comprehensive guide now follows as to what you need to do to put yourself in the best possible position to succeed with your claim; there are many comparable actions in ocean container and air consignments, but there is also enough divergence to need separate consideration of these modes.

CHAPTER 2

An overview of the legal framework for air cargo and ocean cargo liability

2.1 As intimated in the introduction to this work, there is no attempt to deal with the law in detail, other than to give readers a general feeling of how and why claims in transit are processed and viewed.

2.2 A seasoned and knowledgeable marine lawyer may ask for more data in the event of your resorting to enlisting such assistance, but this guide will lead to your creating a comprehensive 'Claim File' fulfilling the vast majority of requirements for the desired result.

2.3 In the small minority of claims on which lawyers need to be enlisted, those lawyers will be able to draw out the necessary and relevant detail.

Air

2.4 Air carriage developed – in historic terms – very quickly indeed from the fateful Wright brothers' demonstration of powered flight in 1903.

2.5 Things had moved on so fast that only 26 years later, sufficient governments around the world felt that an international treaty should be agreed on how compensation and other features of air carriage should be regulated; hitherto, claims against air carriers had been handled in very different ways in different jurisdictions leading to serious inequities and inconsistencies.

2.5 Hence, in 1929 the 'Warsaw Convention' was signed by a large number of States, and each State over the course of several years arranged for the provisions of the Convention to become the law of its land. This Convention covered the carriage of passengers and their baggage, and cargo.

2.6 In 1955, following discontent on the part of various States with the first version, an 'upgraded' version of the Convention was agreed upon, which became familiarly known as 'Warsaw/Hague' and which was signed by many States, and as previously, gradually became law in those countries.

2.7 The first version of the Convention then became familiarly known as 'unamended Warsaw'.

2.8 Some States were or became discontented with both those versions, and in 1999, the 'Montreal Convention' was signed by many States, including a number of those who had refused to participate before – notably, the USA; again, this was made law in most of the signatories' States.

2.9 This version of the treaty has become known simply as 'Montreal'.

2.10 These rules define what is regarded as international air carriage, set down the rights of shippers and consignees, determine the effect and purposes of air waybills,

 DOI: 10.4324/9781003219231-2

provide limitations on the amount of compensation carriers are obliged to pay, and specify time limits for notices of claims, and how long is allowed for a claim to be concluded before it 'dies'.

2.11 In order to determine which version of the Warsaw/Montreal system applies, it is necessary to determine the origin State and destination State of the consignment involved and which version those States have jointly signed; if both are parties to Montreal, then the rules under Montreal are applied.[1]

2.12 The vast majority of States signed and have promulgated Montreal, but one still occasionally encounters situations where an origin State or destination State is not a party to one treaty version or another. One then determines which treaty both the origin State and the destination State have signed, and one can then decide which treaty is applicable.

2.13 There are isolated cases where one State may not have signed any of the Treaties, in which case, it becomes a matter of local law where the claim is submitted which decides how it will be handled.

2.14 However, for our purposes, in the early stages of claims negotiation, the differences between the Treaties tend not to exercise us greatly, and in the text below, the writer will draw out any important differences.

Ocean

2.15 Clearly, ocean carriage has been developing for thousands of years: for instance, since the ancient Egyptians engaged in shipping by sea, it can be supposed that they had some rules about this activity, although none has been found. The history surrounding the development of laws since those days is fascinating in itself, but not within the scope of this book.

2.16 From our point of view, the international treaties which are relevant are the 'Hague Rules' agreed in 1924, the 'Hague/Visby Rules' agreed in 1968, and the 'Hamburg Rules' agreed in 1978.

2.17 A fourth set (the 'Rotterdam Rules') have been produced but it will be many years before they have any practical effect on maritime claims as the ratification process has proved to be particularly slow.

2.18 Each of these conventions sought to fill in gaps that existed previously, to cover all contracts of carriage as well as bills of lading, and to permit carriers to incorporate these rules into their contracts or bills by referring to them specifically.

2.19 Whilst comparable air cargo rules had a relatively 'easy' ride in becoming law in the various States adhering to them, the situation is far more complex in relation to ocean cargo rules.

2.20 The Hague and Hague/Visby rules are commonly encountered in our sphere: as an example, France operates both regimes, applying Hague/Visby to all outbound shipments, and Hague Rules if the consignment comes from a Hague Rules State. Belgium applies Hague/Visby to inbound and outbound consignments.

---

1 The Carriage by Air Act 1961 sets down the rules in the UK. (The act may be dated 1961, but it has been amended as necessary, as is often referred to as 'the Carriage by Air Act 1961 – as amended'.)

2.21 A further example is that some countries, notably in South America, have never adhered to any of the 'Protocols', but generally either Hague or Hague/Visby is incorporated into contracts of carriage.

2.22 In very general terms, you will routinely encounter Hague and Hague/Visby Rules; occasionally, the prospect of proceeding under Hamburg Rules will arise, but the need to consider this will, as like as not, arise only if you are obliged to seek legal advice in the event of a breakdown in negotiations with a carrier.

2.23 The above exposition will appear a little naïve to the seasoned marine lawyer and does require some amplification.

2.24 In general terms, the applicable law is either one that is specified for this purpose in the contract of carriage, or it is effectively determined by the Court hearing the dispute, usually on the basis of being the law with which the contract has its closest connection.

2.25 A carrier is generally enabled to choose its own jurisdiction which need not be the Court of its home country: thus, a good number of carriers not based in England choose the English Court, others France, and yet others Germany. This is by way of a clause in the contract of carriage which identifies which Court or Tribunal is to hear the dispute; this 'jurisdiction clause' will generally state the law that is to be applied as, curiously, a claim can be heard in one country which is obliged by the contract to apply the law of another country.

2.26 A further complication is that one jurisdiction will insist that the rules adopted by the State in which the contract of carriage was concluded are applied, whereas in other jurisdictions, the law of their land applies one or other of the sets of rules.

2.27 It can be bewildering to determine the correct position, but potential difficulties do not tend to make their appearance until and unless negotiations between carrier and claimant break down, and a claimant is obliged to seek legal representation with a view to litigation.

2.28 It is at this point that the claimant, who, for instance, may be situated in the Netherlands, finds that it should instruct lawyers in England. Large importers moving thousands of containers and thus, by the law of averages, having more claims than others, may well find themselves having to be represented by lawyers in several different States in order to progress their various claims.

2.29 There is no realistic prospect of a Dutch claimant persuading a carrier whose bill of lading or sea waybill jurisdiction clause provides for the German Court to agree to litigation in the Netherlands for the claimant's convenience.

Hamburg Rules

2.30 General acceptance by the trading nations of the world of the Hamburg Rules for international carriage by sea would constitute a huge breakthrough in the reform of the law of international carriage.

2.31 Unfortunately, very few States have adopted them, and the instances where such is applicable appear, consequently, to be very limited, and, accordingly, no worthwhile guidance on these Rules can be included in this work.

2.32 Should a claimant encounter these being used by a carrier because they are contractually or compulsorily applicable to a claim, it is appropriate to consult a marine lawyer to determine the claimant's actual prospects for progressing its claim.

2.33 These rules are shown in the annexes of this book for interest, and for future reference should they begin to be adopted by more States.

CHAPTER 3

Detailed actions after discovery of the loss

The question of abandonment

3.1 This is intimately connected with the question of salvage and mitigation which is dealt with in more detail below; however, the point is considered briefly since it obviously arises prior to taking delivery of your products.

3.2 A decision to abandon a consignment must be approached with great care, as it is seldom in your interest.

3.3 Clearly, an asparagus consignment lost by an airline for ten days cannot be conceived of as being at all marketable; a container of scallions delayed for three weeks falls into the same category.

3.4 The premise must be that it is beyond question that the product could possibly have survived in sufficiently good condition to permit of marketing to some degree.

3.5 Yes, it is always a judgement-call, but you must be very clear about it, because it raises the possibility that your entire forthcoming claim could fail.

3.6 If the carrier is reasonably able to argue that the consignment could have been subject to salvage to some degree, but you failed to carry this out, it follows that the salvage proceeds were never established and hence it becomes impossible to calculate what your loss should have been; this would potentially result in a complete failure of the claim, or at very least detailed argument as to what 'mitigation' of loss should have been carried out.

Delivery signatures on collection and receipt

Air

3.7 There is often significant resistance by airline warehousemen to permitting your driver to add a clause to the delivery signature in the Airline's Register recording that there is damage to the consignment.

3.8 It is not always clear why there is this reluctance, but it is seen to arise when, for instance, a driver detects unusual levels of heat being given off by the packages, or perhaps a malodour. The warehousemen may consider that since there is no visible damage to the cartons there is no justification for a claused signature. However, it also occurs when there is visible damage, and this is puzzling.

3.9 Intimidation on the part of warehousemen is known, and there is little that a driver can do about this, and protests seldom make headway, and can be counter-productive by creating the potential for hostility and deliberate non-cooperation when the driver must return for subsequent collections.

 DOI: 10.4324/9781003219231-3

3.10 However, you can take comfort from the law which applies to this aspect of the situation.

3.11 A clean signature is not proof of sound condition at the time of delivery,[1] and conversely, neither is a claused signature conclusive proof of damage, of course.

3.12 Thus, the driver's best course of action in these difficult circumstances is to sign 'clean' and take delivery.

3.13 He is routinely given a copy of the Release Note or Removal Authority which he also signs, since there should be multiple copies one of which is intended to be taken by him; on this document there seems to be less resistance to its clausing, but to do so can still be a problem for a driver.

3.14 This document can then be used as *prima facie* evidence of damage if so claused, or solely for proof of time and date of collection.

3.15 On arrival back at your pack-house, you should immediately establish evidence of the damage, usually photographs which are preferably date/time stamped and show the damage, and probed temperatures. If the Air Waybill number is on the cartons, and this shows in the pictures, all the better.

3.16 If your full quality control inspection can be done immediately on receipt this is the best course of action, as it will doubtless record the problems in detail.

Ocean

3.17 The situation on signatures given for ocean cargo appears less problematical than for air.

3.18 Except on the rare occasions when a problem is known prior to collection from the port, such as, for instance, selection by customs who discover hazardous levels of CO_2 probably arising from closed vents, or foul-smelling liquid running out of the container resulting from putrefaction, a clean signature for the container is routinely given by the collecting driver.

3.19 However, on receipt of the container at your pack-house and your discovery of a problem there is no difficulty in adding a detailed clause to the driver's delivery note. It may be your own contracted trucker delivering but it shows a contemporary record of the damage on receipt – such contemporary records are always more persuasive than reports of such at a later stage.

3.20 You should record arrival temperature, and any fluctuations in the downloaded temperature record if there are any, together with the appearance and condition of the products.

3.21 This, then, becomes an important document evidencing receipt in such condition, as well as, of course, time and date of receipt.

Claim notification and invitation to carrier to attend survey

3.22 The writer has included in the annex to this work some suggested wordings for such notices, which can be amended as appropriate.

1 Article 26[1] of unamended Warsaw and Warsaw/Hague, Article 31[1] of Montreal, which make it clear that a clean signature is *prima facie* evidence only of delivery in good condition.

3.23 At the time of creating this work, the almost-exclusive means of communicating notices is by email, and it is occasionally possible to obtain a 'read receipt' for your emails, although many carriers' computer systems administrators prevent such read receipts being sent.

3.24 Accordingly, it is prudent to firstly call up the carrier and establish precisely to whom the notice should be sent, and once sent, monitor it for a response, and if none is forthcoming, call up the carrier again, and make a timed and dated note on your copy of the message of the name of the person to whom you have spoken.

3.25 Direct liaison with the carrier (or its representative) is vital in the case of ocean cargo! Do not omit to do this.

Air

3.26 If a notice of claim is not sent to an airline, when one is required, 'no claim lies against the carrier', and this simply means that the airline has no legal liability, and therefore can reject any later claim, and you will not be able to succeed with it under any circumstances.

3.27 There are differing legal rules about notices of claim to airlines,[2] and time limits for the giving of them, depending on what has happened to the consignment.

3.28 For instance, when damage occurs in transit, a notice is required, but when an entire consignment is lost in transit none is required, although some US-based carriers have been known to argue against this, and sometimes have found support of a Court in the USA.

3.28 When part of a consignment is lost, in many jurisdictions this is defined legally as 'damage', and a notice within the time limits for damage is thus required.

3.29 Either seven or fourteen[3] days from delivery are allowed for damage, including partial loss, and twenty-one for delay, and, finally, in the case of damage, including partial loss in transit, the failure to give notice of claim in time or at all renders the airline free from having to deal with any claim.

3.30 Accordingly, the only prudent strategy is to forget about these time limits and give absolute priority to the giving of notice, which will simply prevent you falling foul of these rules.

3.31 The one important variation, and something to be particularly aware of, is when a consignment is delayed, and it finally arrives damaged. If you have given notice of loss or delay, on receipt and confirmation of damage you must give a second notice citing actual damage, because if you do not, the carrier is entitled to declare that your notice was anticipatory and not valid.[4]

---

2 See annex for an example Notice of Claim to an Airline.

3 Unamended Warsaw, seven days under Article 26[2]; Warsaw/Hague, fourteen days under Article 26[2]; and fourteen days under Montreal Protocol, Article 31[2].

4 Although from a Netherlands decision, it is submitted that a carrier would use this decision elsewhere as grounds for a rejection: *J W Peters-Maarse h.o.do.n. World Trading v BA (Amsterdam 13 May 1987), [1988] Sc hen Sch 213.*

3.32 If the only notice a carrier has is for delay or presumed loss, and the claim becomes a claim for damage, then the carrier is entitled to hold that it has not been put on notice of such a claim.

3.33 At this point, it should be noted that anyone can give notice of claim when acting for either shipper or consignee: there have been instances where an air carrier has advised that only the shipper or consignee named on the air waybill can give such notice, but this is simply wrong.

3.34 In general terms, if you, as importer and consignee named on the air waybill, take delivery, all rights of claim are vested in you because the benefit of the contract of carriage has passed to you: if it proves appropriate at a later stage, an importer may cede its rights of claim to the shipper.

3.35 Accordingly, it is prudent for an importer-consignee or shipper to issue a notice of claim and include wording to the effect that it is giving notice of behalf of the consignee as well, and vice versa: an example of such wording is included in the annexes.

3.36 A final point on notices of claim: as a matter of course, you must give the carrier an opportunity to inspect the consignment. Failure to make the consignment conveniently available to the carrier will seriously disadvantage you.

3.37 The carrier is entitled to object if they have not been given the opportunity to verify the damage, despite – as above – their almost never arranging inspection for fresh produce consignments.

Ocean

3.38 Article 6 of both the Hague and Hague/Visby Rules provides that notice of claim[5] be given at the time the consignee, or its agent, takes delivery from the carrier, but, of course, with ocean containers this is simply not possible, since any damage – all but the tiniest proportion of containers from which (for instance) the fluids of putrefaction are leaking, or perhaps customs officers on inspection discover something grossly wrong – is not visible.

3.39 Damage becomes apparent normally only on opening up the container and/or unloading it.

3.40 Consequently, in that same Article, it is provided that notice be given within three days of taking delivery.

3.41 However, again in the same Article, if a survey is undertaken jointly by the consignee's and carrier's representatives at the time of receipt a notice need not be given: it is doubtful where a container is delivered to the consignee, and a joint survey then undertaken, that this escapes the need for a notice.

3.42 Accordingly, the principle to be followed is to give immediate notice to the carrier on discovery of the damage; only by this means can a claimant be certain not to fall foul of any of the rules.

3.43 In the event that notice is not given within three days, it is regarded as ***prima facie*** evidence of delivery of the goods 'as described in the bill of lading', viz., in sound condition. This leaves the claimant with the possibility of proving the actual damaged condition

5 See annex for an example Notice of Claim to an Ocean Carrier.

of the cargo on arrival, but they have given themselves an unnecessary evidential 'hill to climb'.

Salvage and mitigation

3.44 The law requires that a party which has suffered loss and has a claim against another party as a result must act reasonably in regard to that loss, and there is further mention of this below.

3.45 Thus, the claimant cannot 'sit in the sun' and claim for 'everything', without making a serious effort to reduce the loss to a minimum. A claimant in the worst case would have its claim denied in total.

3.46 It should be clear enough to see how the question of abandonment of a consignment whilst still in the carrier's possession is tied up with the foregoing point.

3.47 You should look to your surveyor for guidance and assistance on this, but the general principles involved are as follows.

3.48 A typically reasonable effort would entail sorting and repacking and forwarding what is of sufficient quality to the original customer and, of the remainder, selling what may be marketable to a secondary market trader for an 'as seen' price and dumping the remainder.

3.49 What a claimant is not required to do is to take a risk; for instance, incurring expenses of sorting, repacking, and trucking to a secondary market on the 'chance' of possible sales.

3.50 Again, this can be a judgement-call, and you must be ready to defend your decision against contrary arguments raised by a carrier or its surveyor.

3.51 In general terms, the costs incurred in a claimant's mitigation efforts can be added to the claim against the carrier.

Survey and investigation

3.52 Be prudent in your choice of surveyors and be prepared to pay for a good one.

3.53 It is a truly false economy to 'go for the cheapest', if all the surveyor can handle is a simple inspection of the damaged consignment.

3.54 They must be competent in post-harvest technology, and whilst experience is vital, as always, formal qualifications in this field are a strong assurance of that competence.

3.55 It is also important that they have a basic general knowledge of how shipping by air and ocean works, but if they do not, you must be ready to guide them in this regard.

3.56 The survey report is always the foundation of your forthcoming claim, and, thus, it is self-evident that it must be cogent, well-organised, and include all relevant and important facts.

3.57 Your surveyors must also be able to draw valid conclusions from data garnered by them.

3.58 Accordingly, give your surveyor the utmost cooperation and support, and heed their advice in regard to mitigation and salvage, because their mission must be to determine the facts whilst placing you in the best possible position to promote your claim.

3.59 Let us not forget, also, that should your surveyor determine that the facts of the loss obviate a claim against the carrier, and that other factors are at play, this is also a vital service to you which may enable you to eliminate a cause of loss in the future.

Joint and separate surveys

3.60 Clearly, if the surveyors appointed by the carrier and the cargo owner conduct a joint survey, they can agree on the actuality of the damage, and on the cause of the loss.

3.61 This would obviate wrangling between claimant and respondent about damage and cause, but it is an ideal seemingly seldom realised.

Air

3.62 At present, the incidence of surveyors – one acting for you, and one for the airline – jointly inspecting damaged consignments is almost unknown with regard to perishable consignments carried by air but should there be a shift by the airlines in their manner of operating, here is a word or two on the subject.

3.63 The reluctance of airlines to instruct surveyors appears to be to avoid the cost of doing so, and they appear to or purport to rely on the claimant producing a survey report for which the claimant pays.

3.64 This is, of course, unfair in the extreme, because not only does the claimant bear the cost with no certainty about recovering that cost as part of his claim, but also, the airline will, if it can, throw doubt on the survey report thus produced, or interpret other factors involved to its advantage which would have been obviated by a joint survey.

3.65 Having declined the opportunity to have the consignment inspected on its behalf, the carrier cannot be properly justified in throwing doubt on the survey report produced by the claimant, unless of course, there are glaring errors or anomalies in it.

3.66 Should a claim reach Court, that lack of justification would be emphasised, probably putting a stop to unreasonable and unjustified refusal to accept the findings of your surveyor, but more likely such objections could be expected to be lessened or even withdrawn on the advice of the carrier's solicitors should it appear that the case actually may reach the Court.

3.67 Shortly before the completion of this book, a case was decided in the English Court which would appear to create difficulties for defendant airlines in such situations.[6]

3.68 Whilst it obviously remains at the discretion of the Court as to whether to accept a claimant's expert's report, it was held that going forward in cases, a defendant must be proactive and obtain its own expert report to contradict claimants' expert evidence.

3.69 Clearly, the same boon is available to an airline on the occasion that an airline instructs a surveyor to act on its behalf, and the claimant fails or declines to do so.

Ocean

3.70 You can routinely expect ocean carriers to appoint surveyors, but achieving that ideal joint survey remains routinely elusive: good surveyors in demand often have a full diary which does not facilitate joining up with 'opposing' surveyors.

3.71 Sometimes, it appears that surveyors are reluctant to agree to a joint inspection, for reasons which are not always clear, but when it does occur, there remains, of course, the potential for disagreement.

---

6 Griffiths -v- TUI UK Limited [2020] EWHC 2268 (QB).

3.72 There have been occasions when one of the surveyors is seen to be unfamiliar with fresh produce, and this can produce the rather bizarre situation where the surveyor with expertise instructs the other in how to deal with the matter in hand!

3.73 The absence of a joint survey sadly does lead to surveyors rendering reports to their principals which differ in their content, in turn leading to claimant and respondent adopting different positions, and there have been instances where an inexperienced surveyor's report is relied upon by one side or the other despite it not quite making sense in terms of plant physiology and post-harvest factors.

Common causes

Air

3.74 Leaving aside actual loss in transit, the most common cause of loss is temperature abuse, which can occur whether or not the consignment is delayed.

3.75 There are occasional instances of physical damage, when, for instance, the airline has decided at a transhipment point, or even sometimes at origin before loading on board the aircraft, to unload a consignment from a well-stacked aircraft pallet, and reload into containers, the warehousemen appearing to have acted carelessly. On occasion, when the containers have been opened following collection from the destination airport, the cartons can appear to have been thrown into those containers.

3.76 Fewer losses occur when a consignment is carried on one aircraft from origin to destination, and if there is no delay but the consignment is damaged, it is right and proper to consider the possibility that the consignment was delivered to the airline not having been properly packed or pre-cooled.

3.77 However, aircraft holds are known to have been set at wrong temperatures, or consignments have been staged out on the ramps for long periods in hot weather or in freezing conditions; naturally, ascertaining that such events have occurred is not easy, and airlines cannot be expected to readily cooperate and admit such errors.

Temperature abuse

3.78 More often than not, temperature abuse occurs during transhipment, when the consignment is offloaded from one aircraft arriving at a transhipment airport from the origin airport to connect with another aircraft to be carried to its final destination.

3.79 Every carrier has a total legal duty of care towards the cargo, and if the 'dwell-time' at the transhipment point is significant, the airline should be expected to place the consignment in a cold store, and when this does not happen, trouble will inevitably follow.

3.80 Nonetheless, of course, consignments can be exposed to adverse temperatures between delivery to the carrier at origin and the flight departure, and between flight arrival and collection by your driver.

3.81 Dependent on the commodity involved, on delivery to your pack-house you will see dehydration of the product, with its moisture having re-condensed on the packaging, together with shrivelling, rotting, or other manifestation of deterioration.

3.82 Some perishable commodities can stand some ill-treatment, but others are more delicate, and their deterioration can show up as virtual 'melting', and asparagus importers will be familiar with melting and the strong 'feline' quality of its smell when it starts to putrefy.

Delay

3.83 If a consignment is delayed during air transit, it seems that it is particularly vulnerable to damage as a result of temperature abuse.

3.84 If a flight is delayed in arriving at the transhipment point, making it difficult for the airline to connect your consignment to the on-carrying flight, then it may have to remain at the transhipment airport for perhaps 24 hours or more. You are then entirely dependent on the airline placing your consignment in appropriate storage over which you have no control or influence.

3.85 Of course, on rare occasions a consignment is delayed beyond its conceivable shelf-life and inevitably becomes worthless commercially, despite its having been stored at the appropriate temperature by the airline during transit.

Ocean

3.86 As with air, the most common problem is failure of temperature management during transit; to a lesser extent container vents are closed in transit, despite having been in the correct position at the time of container stuffing; and, finally, of course, there are a few instances when cargo is physically lost.

Temperature abuse

3.87 Temperature abuse during ocean transit is a far more complex matter than during air transit.

3.88 However, in general terms, the same type of damage occurs to products as during air carriage.

3.89 Ripening can be triggered in climacteric fruits, such as mangoes, papayas, and avocados, and in non-climacterics, such as grapes, legumes, and root vegetables, including yams, sweet potatoes, and squashes, significant deterioration can be gradually caused, each resulting in light or extensive shrivelling, rots, general putrefaction, and so on.

3.90 Clearly for successful out-turn at destination, the loading of sound quality produce at correct temperature, its correct stowage in the container, and correct settings of the container, and the performance of the container's reefer equipment are all critical.

3.91 The age of the container and hence the condition of its insulation also play a part, and if your surveyor inspects your consignment with the container still present, then he or she must make a note of the data on the manufacturing plate on the container, which usually indicates the date of manufacture. An 'old' container may have insulation which has deteriorated and lost its effectiveness to some degree.

3.92 Sound export quality and correct loading temperature are clearly prerequisites for all fresh produce shipping, but its stowage is a vital factor in successful carriage.

3.93 Containers have varying construction modes to ensure optimum flow of air into and out of all parts of the container, but mainly cooling air is directed through runnels in the container floor, and thus the cartons and pallet stacks must be so constructed to ensure that the flow of air is unimpeded.

3.94 Once the pallets are built and ready to load, they must be positioned in the container so as to ensure that the cooling air can circulate without hindrance.

3.95 Incorrect stowage, or a pallet which collapses, can interrupt circulation, and it is not uncommon in such instances for pallets towards the rear of the container to be deprived of ventilation and cooling air and out-turn in damaged condition, whilst pallets towards the front enjoy the cooling effect and out-turn sound.

3.96 Having ensured all the foregoing, you are now dependent on the reefer equipment performing satisfactorily.

3.97 If your pack house is remote from the port you will need a power source[7] to be mounted onto the container, or for it to be powered from a generator which may be fitted to the tractor unit in order for the temperature and air change to be maintained until it reaches the port.

3.98 It is important to ensure that before the loaded container departs the pack house, power is being supplied to the container, and so far as you can be certain that all is working correctly with the requested carrying temperature being maintained.

3.99 You will also need to check that the vent is correctly set, but you may be prevented from doing this if the GenSet mounted on the container obscures your view of it.

3.100 Whilst the carrier is responsible for setting the container controls, there is also invariably a duty imposed on the shipper, by reason of a clause in the conditions on the reverse of the bill of lading, to verify that the container controls are correctly set – sometimes the wording of the particular condition refers to the shipper ensuring that the container is in all respects fit for the intended purpose.

3.101 In particular, a shipper should check that the 'baffle plate' is correctly positioned; this device is at the front of a container and is responsible for ensuring the cooled air is directed into the floor channels of the container and thus distributed along the length of the container.

3.102 The container will (or should) arrive with the controls set according to the shipper's request, and it appears that no carrier permits a shipper to set the controls or adjust them.

3.103 If the controls are not set correctly, this must be brought immediately to the attention of the carrier, and their instructions sought. It is possible that the carrier will instruct the shipper to adjust the controls under its direction, but more likely its own technician will be instructed to do this.

3.104 The container cannot be allowed to leave the pack-house without all controls having been set correctly and for the container to be working as required – should the vent be masked by a GenSet, then, of course, the shipper cannot check it is set properly.

3.105 The container, having departed from the pack-house, is delivered to the port where it should be powered up on the quay or in the container holding bay until loading on board.

3.106 If power is interrupted or not supplied at any time during this period, there should be an indication when the thermogram is reviewed after the container reaches the consignee's pack-house.

3.107 Temperature maintenance seldom fails during actual transit, although reefer units have been known to break down, of course. However, when a consignment arrives having suffered from temperature abuse, a review of the thermogram can show some strange events, and the baffling question inevitably arises: how can the temperature appear to

7 Known familiarly as a 'GenSet'.

fluctuate when the product in the container is incapable of producing varying amounts of heat at different times as it gradually matures or ripens or even decays?

3.108 So, the next event to be reviewed is how a container has been handled during transhipment at an intermediate port, for it is not unknown for containers not to be supplied with power during the period between discharge from one vessel and loading on board another.

3.109 Again, this type of event should be recorded by the thermograph.

3.110 On arrival at the destination port, the container, once discharged from the vessel, should again be powered up until it is collected. Similarly, failure to do this should be recorded by the thermograph.

3.111 Thus, your thermograph is vital to permit valid conclusions to be drawn about temperature failures during transit which may have led to the damage on out-turn.

Suffocation and CO_2 injury

3.112 It is puzzling that vents apparently are sometimes closed during transit; it is not unusual for the shipper to verify that the vent has been set correctly at the time of container loading, but that on arrival at destination the vent is closed.

3.113 In 1999, a series of 16 containers of mangoes shipped from the Gambia to the UK arrived on different vessels operated by the same carrier with vents closed. This occurred despite the carrier having placed a prominent sticker on each container before delivery to the shipper with temperature and vent setting in accordance with the shipper's request. The fruit was a total loss. Fortunately, the carrier concerned did not attempt to contest the claims.

3.114 Shippers must bear in mind that – as mentioned above – they are responsible for checking the container controls so far as is possible – if this is not a routine point to cover, then introduce a 'tick-box' in your container check-list, so that your operative actually checks this.

3.115 The best thing you can do, as a shipper, is to take photos of the container showing its number, and the vent (as well of the fruit itself and its temperature, of which more below).

3.116 The importer may discover the product is likely to have been seriously damaged on opening the container when that particular and peculiar 'alcoholic' smell is evident. Unless the carrier's surveyor agrees that such damage has occurred, it is strongly recommended that samples of the affected fruit be sent for laboratory analysis to confirm the presence of ethyl alcohol and provide irrefutable evidence of CO_2 injury.

3.117 If the container has had its vent closed for some time, you can anticipate major damage possibly extending to a total loss in these circumstances – more often than not, the whole consignment is tainted, although some carriers' surveyors seem to think that there is a buyer 'out there' for it, but none, of course, can be identified.

Delay

3.118 Understandably, if an ocean consignment is delayed, the delay may in itself threaten the condition and shelf-life of the commodities.

3.119 The carrier may have done everything else according to the book, but the delay, if 'gross', can be damaging in itself; fortunately, such claims appear to be few relatively in number.

Evidencing the container loading

3.120 Consequently, it is wholly in your interest to have clear records of loading the container, and these should consist of the following:

- Photographs of probe temperature of the fruit at the time;[8]
- Photographs of the container showing its number;
- Photographs of the vent – unless obscured by a GenSet, in which case this should be noted;
- Photographs of the stowage;
- Photographs of the location of the thermograph – if possible, showing its serial number so that it can be linked later to what may be seen by the consignee and its surveyor.

3.121 Finally, you should try to ensure that all these photographs are date- and time-stamped – an easily used facility with modern digital cameras, of course.

Pre-shipment condition and temperature

3.122 There are few situations where you can dispense with this vital evidence.

3.123 If the consignment is lost, it naturally becomes unimportant, or if the consignment is so badly damaged for it to be obvious and unarguable that the damage must have occurred during transit, the carrier becomes less able or justified to allege that the consignment started out in bad condition.

3.124 Clearly, as the vast majority of losses involve damage resulting from temperature abuse and delay, pre-shipment evidence becomes irreplaceable, because without it the carrier will allege that it did nothing wrong, and it must have been inherent vice, nature, or quality of the cargo which caused the problem.

Shelf-life tests

3.125 Again, if you are supplying 'multiples', the shipper should routinely be carrying out shelf-life tests, and if these should be produced, they may well show that had the damaged consignment been carried correctly, it clearly should have out-turned at destination in fine condition.

3.126 If you supply multiples, both you and your supplier will have sunk significant resources into achieving certification under the various regimes, and thus, the records which you and your supplier are obliged to keep for this purpose should be immediately available to you.

3.127 What a waste it is not to use them!

The relevance of pre-shipment evidence

3.128 Having proved that the products were sound and properly cooled, you must build on that.

8 Pre-shipment temperature and quality evidence are discussed below, but it is appropriate to combine such evidence with the container inspection records, of course.

The container will almost certainly be loaded at the pack-house with the products being taken from the cold store and placed directly in the container, and so, in particular, temperatures verified at that time are vital.

3.129 However, if you have delivered, perhaps, to an inland container depot for container loading, you must make provision to prove the temperature of the products at the time of handing over and obtain a written acknowledgement of those temperatures from the receiver.

Trip thermographs

3.130 The use of thermographs cannot be emphasised too much, but their interpretation requires understanding of what they indicate.

Air

3.131 The fluctuations in temperature which they show during transit must be reckoned according to their position within the consignment. If it is located deep within a pallet stack it will show a different profile than if it were located towards the outside of the stack.

3.132 Thus, located towards the outside it will be more consistent with actual temperatures to which the consignment has been subjected, whereas located well inside, its correspondence to those actual temperatures will be much weaker and more difficult to interpret.

3.133 At best, the thermograph can pinpoint the event during the air transit where the damage was done, perhaps by relating fluctuations on it to particular stages of the transit, and thus exposure to adverse ambient temperatures during transhipment.

3.134 In particular, as they are always initiated or switched on some time before delivery to the airline, they will also record that the consignment was delivered to the airline at a good temperature and prevent the airline from alleging delivery to them at origin in a too-warm condition.

Ocean

3.135 It is probably best to place two thermographs in a container, one at the rear and one maybe half-way forward: this should enable a balanced conclusion to be drawn about the temperature experience inside the container.

3.136 The same general principles outlined above in the ‘Air’ section immediately preceding can be followed, but with more reliance on the temperatures to which the products may have been subjected during carriage, because all parts of the consignment should have received equal subjection to the ventilation and cooling air.

3.137 If power was not supplied during the journey from the pack-house to the load port, during ocean transit, during dwell-time at a transhipment port, or following discharge at the destination and before collection, this should show up in the thermograms, and together with an analysis of the transit history, valid and worthwhile conclusions can often be reached.

3.138 However, you will also see temperature histories in your thermograms which are puzzling, and which cannot be related to any particular event during the transit, for which you may need the services of an expert in this field.

Analysis of transit history

3.139 Almost all airlines’ and many ocean carriers’ websites allow cargo tracking, which will enable you to print off their record of transit to form part of your permanent file on your loss.

3.140 I have termed this record a 'web-track'.

3.141 The methods of showing tracking on these websites are not standardised.

3.142 The quality of the data on such web-tracks should not be accepted as definitive but should be considered in light of any other data you hold which may show them to be inaccurate or incorrect. In particular, it is apparent from some airlines' web-tracks that entries are left to a clerk who may enter several items of data at once, which are dated at the entry date, and not the actual event date.

3.143 Some airlines' web-tracks contain puzzling multiple and slightly varying entries for the same event, and it is often difficult to draw proper conclusions from them.

3.144 Some airlines show actual times of flight departures and arrivals, of consignment acceptance at origin, and delivery at destination; others show the most basic of information, but in either case, these records are nonetheless often helpful in understanding what may have gone wrong.

3.145 Some ocean carriers similarly show times of container loading and discharge, and on the whole, seem to be able to be relied on for accuracy more so than airlines' data.

3.146 However, such airline transit histories are vital to understanding what may have occurred during transit; sometimes a damaging event can be pinpointed, and at other times you may have only a hint of such an event.

Determination of cause

3.147 Having gathered the above information, it is often possible to reach a reasonable conclusion about the cause of damage to your consignment, and if you have been able to do so, then your claim to the airline or ocean carrier will carry significant weight.

3.148 However, it is just as possible that there are no real indications as to cause.

Air

3.149 In air carriage, perhaps the thermograph simply records steadily increasing temperature throughout the transit – which could be simply because it was placed well inside a pallet stack, and thus was not so sensitive to the rise and fall of temperatures outside the stack.

3.150 Notwithstanding this, if you have proof of delivery to the airline in sound export condition, and at the correct temperature, together with proof of damage when the airline delivered it out at destination, then the airline must answer for the loss.

Ocean

3.151 One seldom sees similar slowly increasing temperatures during ocean carriage, but a history showing various fluctuations leads inevitably to a suspicion of general inconsistency of the reefer equipment operation and that perhaps it was faulty.

3.152 Perishable products do not give off varying amounts of heat as they ripen or rot: the amount of heat given off during transit may gradually increase, but it cannot fluctuate over short periods – it is physiologically impossible. Consequently, if 'see-sawing' temperatures are seen in the thermogram, the only valid conclusion is that it was not the cargo which caused them, and it could only have been external factors related to the performance of the reefer container.

CHAPTER 4

Documentation gathering

4.1 Apart from the data described above, it will always be necessary to gather together the following documents which you will need to present to the carrier. Each has a function – minor or major – in the chain of evidence, and the airline and ocean carrier are entitled to view them.

4.2 Most importantly, should it eventually prove necessary to litigate your claim, you will almost certainly be ordered by the Court to produce all the following documents, and consequently, it is the best policy to attend to these requirements at the beginning of the process, rather than spend a frustrating time digging through your archives at a much later date.

Booking request and carrier confirmation (ocean only)

4.3 This is vital to confirm the carrying temperature and vent setting requested by the shipper.

4.4 This information may subsequently appear on the bill of lading, or sea waybill, and all well and good if it does, but sometimes not all that information appears thereon, and it becomes necessary to prove the request made to the carrier, because the carrier may subsequently deny that such a request was made.

4.5 The carrier's original confirmation of receipt of those requests should be sought from the shipper, which will further support this point for you.

Supplier invoice

4.6 Whilst airlines and ocean carriers will sometimes attempt to link the values shown thereon to any claim settlement, be assured that very seldom can they maintain this position as will be explained below.

4.7 Airlines cannot succeed in such an argument, but under French law, for ocean cargo claims, the measure of damages on a consignment originating from a country which is not a party to either Hague or Hague/Visby Rules is the shipper's invoice, dependent on the form of the bill of lading or sea waybill and in the absence of a carrier's conditions which provide otherwise.

4.8 (At the time of writing, the writer is actively engaged with associate lawyers in France in appealing this French precedent on several claims.)

4.9 In almost all other claims, this invoice supports your entitlement to pursue the claim as the cargo owner and does not relate to the value to the consignee of the consignment.

DOI: 10.4324/9781003219231-4

Packing list or load list

4.10 If a suppliers' invoice refers to only one commodity, or otherwise lists in sufficient detail what is in the consignment, a packing list will be unnecessary.

4.11 If this is not the case, then you must include with your claim the packing list which accompanied the consignment, so that the airline can examine in detail what was in the consignment when considering the claim.

Health documents

4.12 These comprise phytosanitary certificates, conformity certificates, and anything else which may attest to the 'health' of the commodities.

4.13 However, do not regard these documents as proof of marketable quality.

Certificate of origin, movement certificate EUR.1

4.14 These assist in showing that the consignment was exported and imported in a legal manner; if it were not, then the customs authorities would, of course, refuse entry.

4.15 Nonetheless, such documents are expected to be produced to carriers when submitting claims.

Air waybill

4.16 This is clearly a central document in a claim because it evidences the contract of carriage, and consequently, the rights of claim.

4.17 Whilst the airline obviously must have its own copy you must include it with your claim.

4.18 This document shows all the relevant details of the shipper, the consignee, the cargo, and the origin and destination.

4.19 Amongst other data, it should show the booked flights, and 'handling information', the latter often indicating the temperature at which the airline should be holding the cargo – however, there are often omissions of these data.

Air cargo consolidations and house air waybills

4.20 Occasionally, you will encounter a 'house' air waybill, which indicates that a forwarder has acted as a 'consolidator'.

4.21 The forwarder has gathered together two or more consignments and treated them as a single consignment so far as the airline is concerned: the forwarder executes a master (airline) air waybill showing itself as the shipper and the consignee as its agent at destination with whom the forwarder works: simultaneously, it issues a house air waybill showing itself as the carrier and showing the actual shipper and consignee. The forwarder may even have only one consignment, but still issues a house air waybill, together with a master/airline air waybill.[1]

4.22 In these cases, the forwarder charges its client at a certain level of freight and is able to pay the airline a lower rate of freight, thus enabling it to secure a profit margin.

1 Such a consignment is colloquially known as a 'back-to-back'.

4.23 There are certain implications for the way in which claims are handled, but in general terms, an airline will consider the claim, sometimes requiring only a cession of rights[2] from the forwarder to enable the actual consignee or shipper to pursue the claim, of which more below.

Ocean bills of lading and sea waybills

4.24 Again, these are central documents evidencing the contract of carriage and thus containing vital data in relation to that contract, as in the air waybill.

4.25 Whilst there are strict and complex legal rules concerning bills of lading, these seldom come into play in the fresh produce shipping sector, because shippers often provide an 'express release' effectively relieving the carrier of the onerous duties upon it in regard to regular bills of lading for other commodities.

4.26 Sea waybills are becoming more common with fresh produce which are not subject to the same strict rules as bills of lading.

4.27 These documents establish *prima facie* who has the right of claim against the carrier.

4.28 They also routinely carry vital information concerning container settings.

House bills of lading

4.29 This is a document created by a transport intermediary such as a freight forwarder or a 'non-vessel owning contract carrier' (NVOCC).

4.30 The house bill of lading represents an acknowledgement of the receipt of goods to be shipped.

4.31 Accordingly, it represents some evidence of the nature, quantity, and condition of the goods on loading in the same way as the bill of lading issued by the ocean carrier.

4.32 However, the contract of carriage for the goods will normally be contained in or evidenced by the bill of lading issued by the ocean carrier rather than the house bill issued by the intermediary.

Airline release note, removal authority, or airline delivery order

4.33 When your driver collects your consignment from the airline, he is required to sign a delivery note (as well as, in some cases, a register held in the airline warehouse).

4.34 In most cases, the delivery note will be some form of 'release note' – or 'removal authority' if you are a 'customs approved warehouse'.

4.34 If your driver had concerns about the cargo and was able to sign 'claused' this will be very important to your case, and, if not, it will show the time of collection as well as the date, of course, and this may enable you to show no appreciable interval of time between collection from the airport and confirmation of the damage at your facility.

4.35 Whilst a driver collecting a sea consignment from a port signs for it, a copy is routinely not produced to the consignee and thus a consignee is not in a position to include it as part of the file.

---

2 Examples of cession of rights wordings are included in the annex hereto.

Goods inwards records

4.36 This can be a useful piece of evidence showing diligent checking in of the consignment and hopefully the time, again showing no appreciable lapse of time between collection from the airline or port and arrival at your pack house.

First inspections/quality control records and photographs

4.37 This is one of the most important items of evidence, proving that you have a detailed and comprehensive system for inspecting the products, demonstrating your competence. Combined with a competent professional survey, it puts beyond reasonable doubt that the damage was actual.

4.38 When a consignment arrives in an outwardly good condition, or the damage is limited to part only of the consignment, your own quality control inspection is of paramount importance and will always assist your surveyor in carrying out their independent inspection.

4.39 Notwithstanding this, it is to be understood that if a consignment arrives in an obviously very bad way, requiring only independent verification of condition by your surveyor, then there is little point to undergoing the normal quality control inspection routine.

The surveyor's report

4.40 The surveyor's report should be the foundation of your claim.

4.41 To repeat the point, your choice of a competent surveyor is paramount, and trying to save money on this service is a false economy.

4.42 Having produced all the listed documents and data to your surveyor, it is to be hoped that he or she should now be in a position to produce a comprehensive report taking into account all known facts and arriving at a conclusion which should strongly support a forthcoming claim against the carrier.

4.43 It is perfectly reasonable for the surveyor to discuss with you, if necessary, the conclusions at which he or she has arrived, to ensure understanding.

4.44 He or she should have liaised directly with you on the matter of salvage and alternative sales if possible, and to have included details of such salvage in their report, if this is practical.

4.45 On rare occasions, no valid conclusions can actually be drawn as to cause, in which case, of course, it will be difficult if not impossible to pursue a claim, if you are unable to prove that you actually have a case against the carrier.

4.46 However, a clean bill of lading in the hands of a third-party consignee provides a strong legal argument that the damage occurred in transit when the shipper is able to prove the actual sound condition of the cargo on loading.

4.47 Finally, the surveyor may conclude that the carrier is not at fault, and that perhaps there was something wrong at the pre-shipment phase which made a loss in transit more or less inevitable. This is always disappointing for both exporter and importer but is nonetheless a valuable service enabling operational corrections to be made, and enabling them to be more confident in the success of subsequent consignments.

4.48 Thus, the report should comprise a strong and cogent narrative setting out:

- The relevant facts related to the consignment, including an account of the transit;
- Where and when the inspection was carried out;
- Identity of the carrier's surveyor, if known in case of non-joint survey; or details of the joint inspection;
- A detailed analysis of the thermogram;
- A detailed and clear account of the inspection;
- A reasoned conclusion as to the cause of the damage;
- Comments about salvage if applicable.

4.49 Ideally, a surveyor would also determine the extent of the loss, but it is accepted that this is not always practical or possible where a shipment is made up of multiple and differing packs of product. The consignment may require repeated sorting and repacking before a final loss tally can be arrived at, and, clearly, the surveyor cannot oversee this.

4.50 Attached to the report should be the following, as far as is possible, and it is worthwhile listing them in chronological order, which aids understanding as the report is reviewed:

- [Ocean only] booking request and confirmation;
- Supplier's invoice;
- Supplier's packing or load list;
- Pre-shipment quality and temperature record;
- Phytosanitary certificate, or equivalent;
- Certificate of origin, or, similar;
- Air waybill, ocean bill of lading or sea waybill;
- Delivery signature at airline, or endorsed receiving signature for an ocean container;
- Goods inwards record;
- Quality control inspection together with your photographs;
- Notice of claim and carrier acknowledgement;
- Survey photographs.

CHAPTER 5

The legal rules determining for what you can claim

The central principle of *restitutio in integrum*

5.1 Unsurprisingly, there is an extensive body of law dealing with how much a claimant is entitled to claim in varying circumstances, but to avoid over-complication, we will deal only with the normal guidelines applicable to damages arising in our context.

5.2 The central principle is the Latin term *restitutio in integrum*, which literally translated means 'Restoration to the whole, viz., uninjured, state'.

5.3 Under English law damages are said to be compensatory in nature. Accordingly, the established law on the 'measure of damages' has, as its general aim, to put the claimant into the same position as it would have been in if the contract had been performed without breach.

5.4 At the risk of over-simplification at this point, as an importer, you are entitled to base your claim on arrived-sound market value,[1] viz., the price at which you could have sold the consignment, had it arrived in sound condition. However, it must be borne in mind that there may be some exceptions to this general rule. As previously mentioned, in France, where a consignment is shipped by ocean from a country not adhering to either of the main international rules, compensation will be limited to the value of the exporter's invoice.[2]

5.5 As an exporter you are entitled to base your claim on your selling price to the importer[3], plus freight if you paid it and did not include it in the selling price. In some situations, there may be other expenses which you may have incurred which may qualify to be considered, which point is referred to below.

5.6 It necessarily follows from this principle, having established the arrived-sound market value of the complete consignment, a claimant is entitled to:

- Receive settlement of that amount in full if the consignment is entirely lost;
- If the consignment is damaged, and if it is able to salvage some of the consignment and sell it, or sell the complete consignment at discounted price, it should

1 Also see 'Arrived-sound market value (ASMV)' below.

2 Subject, of course, to the result of appeals currently in process.

3 A word of warning – should you be involved in trucking in Europe under the terms of the CMR rules, the principle of using ASMV is not applicable, as the CMR rules lay down how claim values are to be calculated.

 DOI: 10.4324/9781003219231-5

receive the difference between the full sound selling price and the actual amount raised;

- It is additionally entitled to claim for expenses directly and unavoidably arising from the loss.

5.7 Additionally, please note that the Court would generally not allow a claimant to escape from what would have been a bad bargain; for instance, if, for some reason, your damaged imported consignment could never have been sold in the first place for the prevailing sound price, the Court would not rule that a carrier must compensate you for that prevailing price.

Attempts to derogate from this principle

5.8 In the conditions on the reverse of several major ocean carriers' bills of lading you will see a provision actually stating, for instance, that they are liable only for 'cost and freight'.

5.9 Occasionally, an airline will attempt to settle at a value based on cost and freight, viz., the value shown on the supplier's invoice, plus the freight charges. However, since the vast majority of airlines use a standard IATA[4] air waybill contract wording, no provision comparable to that employed by some ocean carriers appears in airlines' air waybill contract conditions.

5.10 Simply, an airline or an ocean carrier attempting to apply such ideas is generally prevented by law from doing so where one or other of the relevant international treaties applies. (However, to repeat the point again, one or two jurisdictions, when dealing with ocean claims, hold compensation to the supplier's invoice value, even when applying either of the primary sets of rules.)

5.11 With reference to the chapter above on the legal framework for air and ocean cargo liability:

- Firstly, there is no reference to the calculation of damages within the international treaties and statute laws dealing with air cargo, and an airline cannot set out its own rules for such calculation in contravention of the legal precedent outlined above, viz., arrived-sound market value.

  (These treaties and laws apply to almost all air carriage, with very few exceptions.)

- Secondly, although definitions of arrived-sound market value can be found in international treaties and laws dealing with ocean cargo,[5] and whilst there is no specific reference to calculation of damages, *prima facie* an ocean carrier is similarly and generally not entitled to enforce any contrary provision in its conditions.

4 International Air Transport Association; the Airlines' Trade Association.

5 For example, Article IV 5(b) of the Hague/Visby.

(These treaties and laws apply to the majority of ocean transits, and, thus, on occasion, it can be difficult for an importer untrained in these matters to determine the correct situation – however, if a carrier responds in a manner not in accordance with the generally understood position, a claimant is, of course, entitled to ask for an explanation, following which, of course, legal guidance can be sought on the point.)

5.12 The principle is, of course, that since the treaties, set down no methods for calculation of sound-arrived-value (SAV), claimants are – at first sight – entitled to calculate their damages according to the laws of their land. However, in Hague/Visby rules there is a commentary about what SAV means, which is referred to in the next chapter.

5.13 If a carrier attempts to apply a cost and freight calculation to the compensation it has to pay out, it generally falls foul of provisions within those treaties which prevent it doing so.[6]

5.14 Reverting again to considering the majority of cases, of course, a carrier is not prevented from arguing about the meaning of arrived-sound market value in the context of a claim in the particular place where their goods are discharged; ocean carriers regularly raise the point, but airlines seldom do so.

Damages in contract and damages in tort

5.15 The foregoing deals with damages arising from breach of contract.

5.16 On rare occasions, you may find yourself unable to proceed with a claim against a carrier, because a party only incidental to but unconnected with the contract of carriage and not an agent of the carrier has caused the damage.

5.17 This situation may arise also where a house bill of lading is involved, and for various reasons it may have proved impossible to 'pin down' the responsible carrier, which alleges that it is not obliged to deal with a claimant since the claimant has no connection with the underlying bill of lading or sea waybill.

5.18 The term 'tort' thus relates to claims for damages caused to a party by a second party where no contract exists between them, and this particular aspect of claims is beyond the scope of this book.

5.19 There are different rules governing how action under this principle is to proceed: this aspect of claims in the fresh produce shipping field is seldom encountered, but, if it should be, it may be difficult to know how to proceed in such circumstances without instructing experienced solicitors to assist, and, accordingly, this section is intended to simply make you aware of the principle.

Interest on damages

5.20 Whilst, in principle, you are entitled to claim for interest on your losses, in practice, you are extremely unlikely to persuade a respondent carrier to pay it – at least, in negotiations prior to the commencement of any legal action.

5.21 A Court judgement in your favour might well include an item of interest; alternatively, it sometimes happens during the course of litigation, that a carrier comes to accept

6 In ocean carriage, Hague and Hague/Visby – Article 3.8; in air carriage, Warsaw and Warsaw/Hague – Article 23 and Montreal – Article 26.

that it cannot expect to succeed in its defence, in which case it seeks through its own legal representation to persuade you to let the Court case terminate, in which situation your 'price' for agreeing to this may well include an item of interest (in addition to a contribution towards the Court fees, and the costs you have incurred with your solicitor) to which the carrier must agree.

Duty to mitigate

5.22 A claimant is under a strict duty to take all reasonable steps to mitigate or reduce its losses, and damages will not be awarded for losses that it could have reasonably avoided.[7]

5.23 As aforementioned, a party having suffered a loss on its consignment during transit cannot simply dump the consignment and claim for its full value without having taken various actions.

5.24 It must check the consignment to salvage whatever it can and sell for best-possible prices and make a reasonable effort to make such sales.

5.25 However, since a claimant is not required to take a risk, should it appear that the costs of sorting, repacking, and trucking salvaged product to an alternative market will exceed any possible return, then the claimant would not be required to take such action.

5.26 In many cases, this will be a 'judgement-call' for you, and you must be ready to justify your decision.

Date for assessment

5.27 The date for assessment of damages is normally the date of the breach of the obligation under the contract.

5.28 In the case of the shipper who is claiming the value of its invoice to the customer/consignee there can be no question about the value of such a claim, as that is fixed by the invoice.

5.29 However, a consignee, who is claiming for a breach of the condition to deliver in the same condition as loaded, will be entitled to claim for the arrived-sound market value,[8] and since such values generally vary, dependent on the time of year, it will be effectively the value of the products on the date of delivery by the carrier.

7 British Westinghouse Electric and Manufacturing Company v Underground Electric Railways Company of London [1912] A.C. 673, 689.

8 Subject to the previously stated exceptions.

CHAPTER 6

Calculation of constituent claim values

6.1 If the cargo is damaged or lost during air or ocean carriage, the claimant should be recompensed for the value of the damaged or lost cargo at the time and place of delivery or when it should have been delivered.[1]

6.2 This is the arrived-sound market value (ASMV) less arrived-damaged market value (ADMV) rule.

6.3 The ASMV rule has been followed in English law in a number of cases, where the Courts have held that where goods are not delivered by the vessel contracted to carry them, the damages will be the market value of the goods when they should have arrived, less the sums which the cargo owner would unavoidably have had to pay to get them.[2] This establishes the date of assessment referred to above.

6.4 As above, damages are compensatory in nature and the consignee is entitled to receive their profit element, the loss of which flows directly from the breach of the obligation to deliver the goods in the same condition as when loaded.

6.5 However, other additional consequential losses, e.g., loss of reputation, loss of future business, are generally not recoverable, which is supported by law, and almost certainly will be excluded by provisions in the air waybill conditions, and the bill of lading or sea waybill conditions. Any such indirect losses would have had to have been within the reasonable contemplation of the parties; if not, such losses would be 'too remote' to be recoverable.

6.6 A spreadsheet has been included in the annex, which, with suitable formulae entered therein, should make your final calculations straightforward; it is a basic document, which you should use as a guide only, adapting and changing it to suit your particular situation. (It is a simple matter to create the necessary formulae to be entered in the various cells.)

6.7 It represents a good starting point for you.

Arrived-sound market value (ASMV)

6.8 The reference above to the term 'market value' used in various Court cases indicates that consideration must be given to what constitutes market value.

1 Note however, that the place of delivery is where the carrier delivers the consignment to the consignee or its agent, and not where the consignee receives it; accordingly, there are implications which are explained in the next section.

2 Rodocanachi v Milburn (1886) 18 Q.B.D. 67 and The Texaco Melbourne [1994] 1 Lloyds' Rep. 473HL.

 DOI: 10.4324/9781003219231-6

6.9 Legal precedent was set when the Court agreed with the claimant's assessment of the damages, which referred to prices 'achieved' for damaged and undamaged goods, as;

> ...being the difference between the price per kg for a particular claimed shipment and the average price per kg for the non-claimed section and applied the difference between the two to the total weight of boxes claimed for that shipment to arrive at the claimed diminution in market value.

6.10 It has also been held by the Courts that claimants would be most fairly compensated if they received by way of damages the nett amount they would have received from their buyers had the consignment arrived in sound condition.[3]

6.11 Given that experience shows that airlines seldom challenge definitions of market and that ocean carriers routinely do so, it is appropriate at this point to refer to what 'Hague/Visby' has to say about it.

6.12 Article IV 5(b) Hague/Visby reads:

> The total amount recoverable shall be calculated by reference to the value of such goods at the place and time at which the goods are discharged from the ship in accordance with the contract or should have been so discharged.
>
> The value of the goods shall be fixed according to the commodity exchange price, or, if there be no such price, according to the current market price, or, if there be no commodity exchange price or current market price, by reference to the normal value of goods of the same kind and quality.

Proof of arrived-sound market value

The 'supermarket market'

6.13 In the UK, it is beyond dispute that the vast majority of fresh produce imported is sold to supermarkets, and, likewise, it cannot thus be disputed that this is a market in itself.

6.14 It is known that supermarkets negotiate prices with individual suppliers, but there is no means of gathering data to show what prevailing prices are at any one time since individual prices are often considered as confidential.

6.15 It is therefore reasonable and proper to produce example sales invoices for sound product to show what identical but sound damaged product was selling for.

6.16 Alternatively, you can produce your sales price lists showing the prices negotiated with particular supermarkets, if such is available, although you may ask the carrier to confirm that they will regard such price data as confidential.

6.17 These valuation methods are sometimes disputed by ocean carriers, but more often, if forced to settle, they will make a percentage offer to induce acceptance, which enables them to avoid discussions about the correct valuation of damages. So far, in the writer's experience, all ocean carriers with whom he has dealt have avoided such discussions, by inducing claimants to accept less than full settlements rather than undergo long and expensive delays and expenses in achieving equitable results, perhaps because the ocean carriers collectively know that it is an argument which they cannot win.

3 The Ines [1995] 2 Lloyds' Rep 144.

The 'wholesale market'

6.18 Whilst dwarfed by the preceding 'supermarket market', this still exists, and price data is routinely gathered and can be accessed in trade publications, although such reports are hardly exhaustive, and sometimes appear to contain varying prices in different market locations.

6.19 If you sell into these markets, you can prove your selling price by producing copies of the reports showing it.

6.20 However, of course, not all commodities are shown on such reports, and you can then revert to your sales invoices to prove sound prices.

Sales price lists

6.21 Failing each of the above options, it is generally acceptable to produce your standard sales price lists.

Arrived-damaged market value (ADMV)

6.22 In order to calculate damages in relation to damaged goods, the market value of the damaged goods must also be ascertained.

6.23 It is self-evident that it is very unlikely that there is an available actual market for damaged goods.

6.24 Thus, when damaged products are actually resold, the resale price will almost always be accepted by carriers as evidence of that 'market' price which is also the probable legal position.

6.25 Again, copies of your invoices for these 'salvage' sales must be produced as the necessary proof.

Cost-based quantum

6.26 If all the above fail you, it has been held by the Courts that damages can be based on the claimant's cost price, viz., the market price at the place where the goods were delivered to the carrier, plus the expenses of transit, plus the reasonable profits of the importer.[4]

Directly related expenses

6.27 Expenses which you have incurred as a direct result of the loss which has been caused you should form part of your claim.

6.28 Those expenses must also be reasonable and supported so far as is possible with invoices or acceptable vouchers.

Survey fee

6.29 Since almost invariably it is reasonable and proper to engage the services of a professional surveyor to guide you in a matter with which you may have little experience or expertise, such an expense should be added to your claim. This is to be supported with the surveyor's invoice, of course.

4 O'Hanlan v Great Western Railway (1865) 6 B. & S. 484.

6.30 On occasion, a carrier will dispute that a survey fee can be claimed, but this is incorrect. This view appears to arise from transit insurers' regular activities.

6.31 It is routine for a transit insurer to employ and pay for the services of a loss adjuster/surveyor when a loss arises which may be payable under their policy conditions, and, clearly, this is a regular expense incurred in the normal running of their business.

6.32 When a transit insurer has paid your claim and proceeds to attempt to recover the settlement from the carrier, it would not seem proper for the insurer to reclaim a normal and routine business expense. The carrier is liable to the claimant, and if the claimant's insurer has incurred an expense in the normal running of its business, it has not been incurred by the claimant.

Sorting/repacking

6.33 Many importers have their own pack-houses, and their employees are tasked with this.

6.34 Therefore, a record of the time input required set against the average hourly rate of pay can be included in your calculation; in such a case, you can only produce your own calculation, but if reasonable, there may be no objection.

6.35 Other importers engage contractors for this task, and thus, their contractors' invoices for the work will support the amount claimed for this.

6.36 There may have to be replacement cartons, and the cost of these should be supported with invoices from the relevant suppliers.

Dumping costs and certification

6.37 Worthless product needs to be dumped, of course, and this process is routinely controlled by legal environmental regulations. Packaging materials must be separated from the actual commodities, normally incurring labour costs. Packaging is disposed of relatively easily, but the perishable produce must be dumped according to established local and governmental rules.

6.38 Naturally, costs arise for each of these functions, and you should similarly seek to support those costs with internal costings for labour, and/or invoices from contractors.

6.39 Just as important is reasonable proof of dumping waste product, failing which the carrier will imply that the product actually dumped, was, in fact, sold instead.

Other possible costs

6.40 Having received a damaged or sub-standard consignment, it may require intensive effort by your staff to locate alternative buyers and negotiate sales; and thus, staff time costs are incurred.

6.41 To get your products to alternative buyers you may have to incur haulage costs which would not have been so incurred had there been no problem in the first place.

6.42 Perhaps your consignment incurs extra costs of storage whilst alternative sales are being effected.

6.43 Again, such costs can be properly claimed and supported with vouchers, but, of course, there is no guarantee that carriers will not object to such costs.

CHAPTER 7

Claim submission

7.1 Finally, you have marshalled all your facts and figures.

7.2 You have a first-class survey report, which includes all available data and evidence relating to the consignment and manner in which you suffered the loss, and you have calculated your losses and have the supporting evidence for them.

7.3 It is now time to put all this together and present your comprehensive and well-reasoned claim to the carrier.

7.4 There are some simple rules to follow.

Covering letter

7.5 A long letter of explanation of your claim should be unnecessary if your survey report contains sufficient and necessary facts about the cause of loss, and your quantum is set out clearly and supported by the necessary paperwork.

7.6 You should perhaps include a brief outline of the claim but include any points which – for one reason or another – it has not been possible for your surveyor to include in his or her report.

7.7 In particular, it is sometimes not possible for salvage and mitigation details to be included in a surveyor's report, and thus it becomes necessary to provide an explanation for what you did or could not do in this regard.

Presentation standards and well-ordered attachments

7.8 Whilst only a tiny minority of claims ever reach Court, it is prudent to operate on the principle that everything you submit to the carrier may finish up being scrutinised by a judge.

7.9 Scruffy documents, missing documents, and difficult-to-follow claim submissions will not find favour with the Court, and, whilst a judge is committed to total fairness, you will not create a good impression if he or she is unable easily to understand everything.

7.10 Obviously, the same goes for the carrier to whom you present your claim; do all you can to ensure that the claims handler at the carrier has no difficulty in understanding your case – again, missing or scruffy documents, and unclear explanations will create obstructions and delays to making progress on your claim.

Submission of claims by email

7.11 It seems that at the time of writing, claims can be submitted almost exclusively by email, following the scanning of all the documents constituting the claim file.

DOI: 10.4324/9781003219231-7

7.12 With an email, if you do not receive back an error message informing you that your email has not been delivered to the addressee for one reason or another, you can be reasonably confident that it has made it to its destination.

7.13 One may still encounter difficulties where carriers' computer server file size settings are smaller than desirable, but files can be split into parts. Additionally, with 'pdf' formats for scanned files being almost exclusively used, such files can be reduced in size.

Other methods of claim submission – air cargo claims

7.14 There has also been more than one attempt to construct a 'catch-all' single website tool for the submission of claims to which airlines subscribe; however, they are not necessarily user-friendly. Nonetheless, airlines are promoting the use of these 'tools'.

7.15 The writer's experience of these tools has been somewhat indifferent with some worrying problems, and whilst such a facility would appear to be beneficial in general terms, it may be some time before one is 'perfected'.

7.16 Of concern, there have been a few instances where one of the currently operating websites has appeared to act for airlines which have no connection to that website. On occasion, claimants have been induced to give notice of claim through this website to their cost.

7.16 In particular, with regard to a website tool currently in operation, one can obtain what appears to be an acknowledgement of a submission, and then find that it appears difficult or impossible to chase up for responses. Chaser messages on the website meet with no reaction.

7.17 If you submit your claim via this facility, you should be prepared to follow it up directly with the airline no matter what.

If by post, obtain recorded delivery and why

7.18 It has seemed unnecessary to submit claims by post for some years now, but, if you find yourself having to do so, it is strongly suggested that you use a recorded delivery facility, or have your claim couriered to its destination, which will avoid any question of the carrier not having received your claim.

Ask yourself?

7.19 Finally, on the matter of submissions, it cannot be stressed strongly enough that you should repeatedly ask yourself if you have made everything clear and intelligible.

7.20 If it is not, then you can depend on your claim making little progress whilst the carrier struggles to understand it, and repeatedly asks you for more documents or explanations.

CHAPTER 8

Time limits and time bar protection

8.1 The term 'time limit' refers – in this context – to the giving of notices of claim to the carrier within the specified time limits.

Time limits

Air

8.2 To recapitulate: for air cargo you have 7 or 14 days in the case of damage or partial loss in accordance with Hague, Warsaw/Hague, and Montreal Protocols.

8.3 Nothing appears in those treaties in regard to total loss, and, so, a notice is not necessary. However, bear in mind that carriers' air waybill conditions often show that notice must be given in the case of loss within 120 days, and such has been upheld in some Courts in the USA.

8.4 Consequently, ensure that notices of claim are given immediately upon learning that a loss has taken place – this obviates any difficulties. At the risk of being excessive, and with reference to the preceding paragraph, it is recommended that even in the case of actual loss (non-delivery), notice of claim is given.

8.5 Also, remember that if a consignment has been delayed, and you have given notice, when it is received, and you find that it is damaged, you must give a secondary notice specifying damage.

8.6 In the absence of such timely notices, 'no claim lies against the carrier',[1] which means that the carrier is relieved of all liability and does not have to answer for the claim.

Ocean

8.7 You have three days to give notice from the time the carrier delivers to you or your agent, usually at the discharge port.

8.8 In the absence of such notice, not all is lost, but you are held to a much higher burden of proof – meaning principally that you have to prove, as a matter of fact and evidence, that the damage existed at the time of delivery to you by the carrier.

8.9 You may also suffer difficulty if the carrier has not been afforded a fair and reasonable opportunity to appoint a surveyor to inspect the damage.

1 Article 26.4 of Warsaw/Hague and Article 31.4 of Montreal.

DOI: 10.4324/9781003219231-8

8.10 It is, of course, hoped that you have made the giving of notice an absolute priority so that you never fall foul of these rules.

Time bars

8.11 The term 'time bar' refers to the provisions in the international treaties providing that if settlement of claim is not agreed within two years of the date of the loss in the case of air, and one year in the case of ocean, the carrier escapes liability, and the rights of claim 'die', never to be resurrected.

8.12 Different actions are required dependent on the mode of carriage, as follows.

Air

8.13 It is not unknown for an air cargo claim to still be unsettled when the two-year period expires.

8.14 Perhaps for some reason you did not submit the claim until a long time after the loss took place, or the dialogue between you and the carrier about the claim has been very protracted.

8.15 The wording in the treaties is:

> The right to damages shall be extinguished if an action is not brought within a period of two years, reckoned from the date of arrival at the destination, or from the date on which the aircraft ought to have arrived, or from the date on which the carriage stopped.[2]

8.16 This is unequivocal: it means the claim is extinguished, unless you have issued Court proceedings – such proceedings do not have to be served immediately, but each Court-issued claim form has a 'life' of four months in the English Court, and six months should it have to be served outside English jurisdiction, and since it is unlikely to be renewed by the Court, you almost certainly have to serve it if you still have not reached agreement with the respondent carrier.

8.17 However, of course, at this stage you must have instructed legal representatives who should take care of this point on your behalf.

Ocean

8.18 In regard to ocean, the situation is different.

8.19 The relevant wording is:

> the carrier and the ship shall in any event be discharged from all liability whatsoever in respect of the goods, unless suit is brought within one year of their delivery or of the date when they should have been delivered. The period may, however, be extended if the parties so agree after the cause of action has arisen.[3]

---

2 Article 29.1 of Warsaw/Hague, and Article 35.1 of Montreal.

3 Article 3.6.4 of Hague/Visby – the parallel clause in Hague can be regarded for our purposes as having a similar import.

8.20 If no settlement agreement has been reached with the respondent carrier at the expiration of the one-year period, it is routine and normal to request an extension from the carrier.

8.21 This is generally granted for a three-month period, at the expiration of which you are obliged to ask for another. However, some carriers will grant only perhaps a month by which means they knowingly put the claimant under considerable pressure, of course.

8.22 Failure to obtain an extension will result in the claim 'dying', and it is just as final as missing a time-bar on an air cargo claim.

8.23 If the carrier refuses or fails to grant an extension, then you are obliged to issue Court proceedings (or appoint an arbitrator if the contract of carriage calls for arbitration), but, again, by this stage you will probably have instructed legal representatives who will be advising you on the point, and accordingly taking care that all is done correctly.

CHAPTER 9

The struggle for settlement

9.1 It is difficult at times for claimants to avoid regarding carriers' claims handlers as seeking every possible means to avoid settling a claim, in which the concept of customer relations appears very distant indeed.

9.2 As previously mentioned, there are carriers who act in an honourable way, are courteous and professional in their communications, and accept liability when reasonable evidence is presented.

9.3 Sadly, however, there are a number of carriers who are exceptionally slow to respond to anything, chaser-emails are ignored, and chaser-phone calls are fielded and yield promises of attention to your claim which do not materialise.

9.4 You will experience your evidence being dismissed or ignored, and the carrier's stated defence based on evidence which you cannot persuade them to produce.

9.5 Sometimes, a claimant believes its business to be especially important to the carrier and seeks to capitalise on this, but experience shows that this seldom, if ever, yields any results. A claimant might attempt to go through the carrier's marketing personnel assigned to its account, and those personnel will be very sympathetic and promise to do what they can, but, apparently, they cannot influence the claims department of their company.

9.6 Awaiting results through this medium is little different from awaiting an answer direct from the claims department.

9.7 The premise is that, as the claimant, the burden of proof is upon you to prove your claim, and to persuade the respondent carrier to pay up: the first task appears easy enough, but at base, the second is frustratingly difficult.

9.8 Simply expressed, a carrier does not have to settle your claim until forced to.

9.9 In a good number of cases, only a credible threat of legal action or actual legal action has brought about a result, and even then, the carrier has done all possible to settle for the smallest amount, in the knowledge that a discounted offer might tempt a claimant to settle rather than continue to wait for an indeterminate period to actually reach a result.

9.10 The reality is that the situation is loaded in favour of the carrier, and there is no choice but to accept this.

9.11 It also appears that airlines are a little readier to settle claims at an early stage compared to ocean carriers, whose resistance to settlement can, at times, be extreme.

9.12 Thus, it is perhaps the best policy to start out with an expectation of resistance at every stage of the process, and the following overall strategy is proposed:

DOI: 10.4324/9781003219231-9

1. Present the claim in the strongest possible terms, with a clear conclusion as to cause if possible, supported by clear evidence, leaving as little as possible for the carrier to be able to question;
2. Additionally, ensure that quantum is clearly expressed and fully supported;
3. Press for a substantive answer, and be prepared to field holding replies;
4. Be prepared for your evidence to be ignored or dismissed without explanation;
5. Be prepared to receive repudiations and defences which – in the extreme – appear outrageous and without foundation. Repudiations are occasionally based on poorly understood information about perishable products which are susceptible to rebuttal on sound grounds citing authority, but, again, do not be surprised if this does not appear to sway the respondent carrier;
6. Be prepared for the carrier to 'close up shop' at a certain point – either by declaring that no settlement offer will be made, or simply discontinuing correspondence;
7. Then, if you remain convinced of the merits of your case, consider instructing lawyers. Making such a decision is nerve-wracking for many claimants, in view of the many anecdotal stories of lost cases and big legal costs, but this thorny subject will be discussed below with an attempt at demystification.

9.13 Of course, at any stage of the claims saga, you may decide to instruct lawyers in any case, and there are certainly one or two carriers whose claims handling is so bad that there is little point in waiting for something to happen, and it is prudent to submit the claim and contemporaneously instruct your lawyers to immediately take up the case with carriers or even have your lawyers submit the claim on your behalf with instructions to pursue matters vigorously, and commence litigation at the earliest opportunity. Alternatively, the respondent carrier may be so combative, that no progress can be made, and thus, the only way forward is to 'join the battle' through the medium of lawyers.

Unreasonably delayed responses and refusal to deal

9.14 This is a common problem, routinely encountered by all claimants.

9.15 You will have submitted your claim and wonder why you cannot get a substantive response.

9.16 You may get a fairly early 'holding' response from the carrier and be told that you cannot expect to hear from them for three months whilst your claim is 'investigated', but it is difficult to understand why a commercial sector and airline based primarily on the immediacy of the service involved should take so long to ascertain facts and make a decision.

9.17 A number of airlines head-quartered in the USA have taken this stance, and they appear immovable and may well take considerably longer than that.

9.18 At times, it has been clear enough that the airline as a corporate entity regards its claims handling operation with little respect, presumably since it is a potentially draining cost to the company, and as a result, it is routinely under-resourced.

9.19 Claims handlers regularly complain – almost certainly justifiably – of being under-resourced and thus 'volumed-out' with work and may assure you that they are simply doing their best.

9.20 This may engender some personal sympathy for the claims handler at the time, but as the delay continues, your sympathy proves antagonistic to your interests.

9.21 When a dialogue is finally commenced with the respondent carrier you will also encounter regular delays, and you may wonder why this is happening.

9.21 It could be that you have made such a significant point that the claims handler has been obliged to pass the matter over to the company's insurers, and further delays occur while they consider matters – you may or may not be told that this is happening, of course.

9.22 It could be that the claims handler cannot find an argument against your points of claim or your answers to his or her objections, and refusal to respond at this point is an attempt to discourage the claimant, who finally sees no option other than to instruct lawyers.

9.23 The claims handler is well-aware that the decision to instruct is very difficult for a claimant, and as a result a proportion of claims will actually fall away, where the claimant is discouraged at the prospect of legal action, with its inherent risks and costs.

9.24 As referred to above, you may seek to escalate the matter to a level above that of the claims handler; this has been attempted on many occasions, of course, but it is very seldom effective. The claims handler's manager is under pressure from his superior to avoid settling or to settle at irreducible minimums, and that person is, in turn, under pressure from his superior who may indeed be the financial director or vice president finance for whom claims handling likely has little priority.

9.25 Some carriers will have outsourced their claims handling at any point in the process to loss adjusters or to lawyers; if this happens you can expect further delays whilst they re-examine everything before taking up the matter with you, but at least, you can reasonably expect less-delayed responses.

9.26 The above commentary concerns general attitudes, the possible reasons for them, and the likely events during the claim saga you can expect to encounter with carriers; there now follows an account of many of the responses and reactions you will meet with when a significant dialogue commences with the carriers or their representatives.

The burden and onus of proof

9.27 The burden or onus of proof has evolved through litigation over the years so that it is well understood – it is a central and fundamental aspect of all claims considerations.

9.28 If cargo is delivered to a carrier in sound condition, with a full expectation that it can successfully survive transportation, but is lost or delivered in a discrepant condition, there is immediately a *prima facie* case against the carrier.

9.29 The carrier is then entitled to disprove its liability for the loss or damage by showing that the reason for its non-liability falls within the defences permitted by air or ocean rules.

9.30 Both parties must prove all facts available to them.

9.31 Thus, if called upon, a shipper must prove that the consignment has been properly prepared for transit, because sea waybills and air waybills are not proof of sound condition at the time a fresh produce consignment is delivered to a carrier, unless it can be shown that the carrier inspected the cargo at the time of its acceptance – which is almost unheard of in perishables shipping, of course.

9.32 Of course, if the reason for the loss or damage is patently obvious, such as in actual loss, or, in the case of damage, when, for instance, a reefer container is known to have malfunctioned, then it should be unnecessary for the carrier to seek exhaustive proof of the condition on loading.

9.32 'Clean' bills of lading can be proof of sound condition in various circumstances, but since we are dealing preponderantly with shipper-loaded reefer containers, the carrier has no opportunity to confirm condition, and thus, a bill of lading cannot be taken as proof of shipment in sound condition.

9.33 As above, the claimant must show that it has given notice of claim in a timely manner – required by law for air claims, but not, it seems, necessary for ocean claims where a joint survey has been carried out at the time of delivery by the carrier at destination, thus proving that the ocean carrier was well-aware of a potential claim.

9.34 Neither party is required to prove all the circumstances to the point of absurdity.

9.35 As an example, in recent years, some carriers have resorted to demanding every shipper's document relating to the moment of actual harvesting, right up to loading the container, and declaring that without all of them they will refuse to consider the claim, not caring that the shipper concerned has shipped countless containers with them which have out-turned sound, and that such documentation can run into many pages.

9.36 It is submitted that records of pallet/product temperatures taken at the time of container loading, product inspection records, pictures of the container, the stowage, and the settings of the controls are sufficient in such circumstances.

9.37 In an English law case,[1] the Court made the general point that where a shipper's quality control procedures are well-established and it has a reputation for routinely supplying high-quality products which compare favourably with other similar shippers, the proposition that poor condition at the time of shipment could be the cause of damage on receipt by importers is difficult to accept, since this would mean that similar problems would be suffered by all the shipper's consignments at and around that time.

9.38 Of particular note, and prior to publication of this work, there was a case decided by the Supreme Court in the United Kingdom[2] which clarified the rules on the burden of proof between carrier and claimant, in particular relating to allegations of inherent vice.

9.39 This judgment indicated that it is not an over-simplification to state that if it was established that the cargo was shipped in apparent good condition but was discharged damaged, the burden of proof is on the carrier to show that it did not breach its obligation to take reasonable care.

9.40 Additionally, where the carrier has shown that there may be an exception to liability as provided for within the applicable rules, it is not for the claimant to disprove this, but for the carrier to prove it.

9.41 If, of course, claimants are forced to litigate, they will find themselves having to bolster their proof with whatever other evidence is available; but so, also, will respondents, of course, since each party will be seeking to persuade a judge of the merits of their case.

---

1 Exportadora Valle de Colina S.A. trading as Exportadora Santa Elena & Ors -v- A. P. Møller-Mærsk A/S Trading as Maersk Line [2010] Ewhc 3224 [Comm].

2 Volcafe Ltd & Ors -v- Compania Sud Americana de Vapores SA [2018] UKSC 61.

Delay not involving physical damage

9.42 It is not entirely obvious where the need for a commentary on delay should be located in this study, but, certainly, claimants need to have some idea of where they stand in these issues.

9.43 Again, it is to be understood that the word 'damage' is used in two separate contexts:

- Damage can be losses sustained through physical damage to a consignment, dealt with elsewhere in this study;
- Can be financial damages sustained without physical damage where, for instance, a consignment is delayed long enough for a market to be lost.

9.44 An example illustrating the latter context was where an air consignment of asparagus timed to coincide with the Christmas market arrived delayed at destination on the eve of Christmas day, leaving no time to reach the shops prior to the Christmas break.

9.45 The market for the product effectively disappeared until just before the New Year, and the consignment, whilst viable on the day of arrival, the carrier having apparently cold-stored it correctly while delayed at a transhipment point, effectively became a total loss for the importer since shelf-life determined that it was unsaleable when the market reappeared.

9.46 In this case, fortunately, it was shown that the carrier could not justify failure to load on the booked flight, and the claimant received compensation.[3]

9.47 Such damages will be referred to, for this study, as 'consequential loss'.

9.48 A further example of consequential loss is when a consignment is delayed (again, without physical damage involved) such that the importer (or shipper) loses the expectation of further business of which he had been assured.

9.49 In general terms, losses of this nature are unrecoverable on the grounds that such is not properly foreseeable on the part of the carrier, and therefore, the carrier cannot be aware of and equitably accept the risk as part of its liability. Such losses are said to be 'too remote'.

9.50 With regard to ocean carriage, in the right circumstances under Hague Rules, this type of damage is recoverable since those rules do not refer to them at all. Thus, the *lex fori*[4] applies, and in many jurisdictions, this means that such damages can be claimed.

9.51 Under the Hague/Visby Rules, Article IV 5(b) specifies that 'the <u>total</u> amount recoverable is calculated by reference to the value of such goods at the place and time at which the goods are discharged from the ship', which clearly does not permit consequential damages.

9.52 Article 5 of those rules does permit a carrier to increase any of its responsibilities provided it is shown in the body of the bill of lading – and within a sea waybill governed

---

3 Article 19 of the Montreal Convention provided for the carrier's liability in this case. The carrier conceded the point, and the matter was not litigated.

4 Literally, the 'law of the market', viz., the law of the country where any such case may be brought or decided.

by those rules, as well. However, such a circumstance has not been encountered by the writer.

9.53 The conditions on many bills of lading either exclude liability for delay, or, if held liable, limit such compensation to two or perhaps two-and-a-half times the freight charges.

9.54 In some jurisdictions, the clause to exclude liability for delay where physical damage is caused has been specifically held not to be effective. Thus, it is submitted that such clauses are intended to apply to 'classic' delay problems, involving economic loss, and not to physical damage resulting from delay.

9.55 Thus, the position on delayed ocean carriage under Hague and Visby Rules is not properly and clearly defined, which has led to disharmony between various jurisdictions.

9.56 Where opposition to such compensation is met from carriers, it may be worthwhile consulting qualified marine lawyers who can advise on the particular position which claimants find themselves in.

9.57 However, it must be borne in mind, of course, that it is unlikely that a claimant can contractually obtain better than two-and-a-half times the freight, and this may make the exercise of consulting lawyers uneconomical, a clear illustration of the unequal 'playing-field' tilted in favour of refractory carriers.

9.58 As expressed elsewhere in this study, were Hamburg rules to be adopted generally, many uncertainties would disappear in regard to delay of ocean cargo.

9.59 The vast majority of claimants will not encounter these particular rules in their efforts to obtain compensation, and thus, there will be no detailed exposition of them; suffice it to say, that, in its Articles 5 and 6, the carrier is made liable for delay unless – as under the international air treaties – it can prove that it took all measures that it could reasonably take to avoid the delay and its consequences.

Air cargo

The central principle of a carrier's liability under applicable law

9.60 We all know that in a criminal trial, a defendant is presumed innocent until he is proven guilty.

9.61 The international treaties governing air carriage liability actually reverse that principle: thus, if a consignment is lost, damaged, or delayed, the carrier is presumed to be liable and is obliged to disprove that liability.

9.62 In a 'quid pro quo', the carrier is granted limited liability.

Aspects of entitlement to claim and sue

9.63 It is clear from Warsaw and Montreal provisions that until the consignee pays any charges due and complies with the conditions of carriage, at which point the consignee can require the carrier to hand over the consignment, the shipper remains in control of the consignment.[5]

5 Articles 12 and 13 of Warsaw, Warsaw/Hague, and Montreal.

9.64 In the event that the consignee does not take those actions, the shipper is effectively in a position to claim and sue.

9.65 So soon as the consignee fulfils the above requirements, the rights of the air waybill contract pass to it, which is why abandonment of a consignment for any reason requires the most careful consideration.

9.66 A consignee cannot automatically suppose that abandonment will place responsibility for the consignment back in the lap of the shipper and that it will be free of any further responsibility; and, in any case, the consignee must also take into account the purchase agreement[6] with his supplier, which may require him to pay for the consignment in any case.

9.67 There are circumstances in which parties other than the shipper or consignee shown on the air waybill will be entitled to claim and sue, and under English law,[7] a cargo owner not shown on the air waybill can do so.

9.68 Objections to this precedent have been voiced but, at the time of preparing this work, no challenge to that decision has yet made its way to the Court.

Cessions of rights

9.69 Occasionally, another party, other than the consignee or its direct representative, such as its customs clearance agent, will issue a notice of claim to the airline.

9.70 This appears to occur particularly when a shipper, having knowledge of a loss, and as yet unpaid for the consignment, and naturally keen to protect its interests as far as it can, may intervene with such a notice.

9.71 If the airline is in receipt of notices from both shipper and consignee, it will almost certainly refuse to process the claim until one of the notices is withdrawn, which can usually be done with a simple message from the party thus withdrawing.

9.72 The reality of the situation is that if the consignee has taken delivery of the consignment, then the shipper's rights under the air waybill contract have terminated, and strictly speaking, it cannot claim and sue, but should look to enforcing the terms of sale to the consignee.

9.73 Nonetheless, it is not unreasonable for the airline to err on the side of caution and insist on one of the parties signifying that they withdraw their intention to claim, and, in most of these situations, the airline will insist that a cession of rights be formally issued by the party withdrawing, and an example of the wording which is necessary is included within the annex hereto.

In relation to house air waybills

9.74 Some carriers' claims handlers will simply process a claim from an obvious beneficial consignee as shown on a house air waybill, and others will insist on receiving a form of cession of rights from either or both the shipper or/and the consignee shown on the master airline air waybill.

---

6 All exporters and importers should be aware of and use the provisions of INCOTERMS, which can be sourced on the Internet.

7 Gatewhite Ltd v. Iberia Lineas Aereas de España SA [1988] 1 QB 326.

9.75 There are some interesting discussions to be had about the actual situation, but it is practical and hopefully straightforward to obtain a cession of rights in such cases, because that should eliminate any need to discuss such issues with claims handlers.

9.76 It is clear also that some claims handlers do not have full understanding of these issues in the first place, and the provision of a cession of rights should again eliminate any difficulty here.

Objections to quantum

9.77 You can expect to be challenged on the constituents of your quantum.

9.78 As above,[8] whilst attempts are made to do so, a carrier generally cannot maintain a settlement offer based on cost and freight, or some variation thereof.

9.79 Airlines do not appear to challenge the definition of the 'market' on which you base your ASMV, but ocean carriers are very ready to do so, insisting that it can only be the wholesale market.

The 'market'

9.80 Damages must be reasonably foreseeable by the carrier and in the environment of fresh produce shipping, it has been explained to ocean carriers concerned on many occasions, for at least 30 years at the time of writing this book, that there exists the 'supermarket market'[9] and that it dwarfs every other market in the UK.

9.81 Accordingly, it is not possible for them to maintain that damages related to the price levels in this market are not foreseeable.

9.82 Nonetheless, they purport to deny the reality of the supermarket market; clearly, it is a matter of time only before a case is eventually brought before the Courts to settle the question, and it is difficult to see what defence can be mounted by the carriers.

Survey fees

9.83 The argument is sometimes advanced by carriers that survey fees are not an allowable expense within a claim.

9.84 However, it is submitted that if surveyors are employed by the consignee to independently verify the actuality of damage, as most airlines demand, to calculate the extent of loss and to suggest ways to keep the loss to a minimum, then their fees should the responsibility of the carrier.

9.85 The airlines who take a contrary position are probably influenced by the use of loss adjusters and surveyors by insurance companies, the expense of which is an operating cost of those insurers, and which cannot be charged against the carrier.

9.86 At the time of writing, it is customary for airlines to not instruct surveyors to act for them when a fresh produce consignment is reported damaged, and it appears that they take unfair advantage of the consignee's unavoidable need to provide independent evidence of damage.

9.87 Thus, the consignee is forced to incur the cost of survey, and the airline relies on the consignee's survey report without any cost to itself – but it still feels free to undermine, criticise, and deny the facts reported in that report.

8 See 'Quantum' and 'Attempts to derogate from this principle' above.

9 See 'Proof of arrived-sound market value' above.

All other expenses

9.88 Arguments may be raised on whether such expenses qualify for consideration, and in regard to the amount involved.

9.89 The response to the qualification of the expense is to restate why it was reasonably and necessarily directly related to the loss.

9.99 The response can only be left to your judgement and justification; where a contractor has billed you for such an expense, there should be no effective argument, but where you have incurred and costed an internal expense, then you may have to restate its rationale, or if it appears to you to facilitate the carrier's consideration, modify the amount, or concede it.

Defences – and countering them

Contributory negligence

9.100 Before launching into specific defences which may be offered by carriers, claimants should be aware of certain general principles generally defined as 'contributory negligence'.

9.101 In our context, an example of this would be if a shipper failed to properly cool its consignment for transit, and delivered it to the airline in this condition, or loaded it into a reefer container similarly.

9.102 Ocean carriers will readily point out that a reefer container is not designed to remove field heat, and whilst temperature of the product may be gradually reduced to the requested carrying temperature during transit, by the time it reaches that temperature, it may already have become advanced, possibly ripened, and probably unsuitable for its originally intended market.

9.103 Clearly, for an airline moving a consignment as quickly as possible between origin and destination with a possible few hours only at a transhipment point, the issue of field heat is not necessarily relevant.

9.104 Other 'contributory negligences' encompass failure to provide proper packaging with inadequate ventilation or failure to stow correctly in reefer containers, such that the circulation of cooling air is frustrated, and readers can no doubt think of other instances.

9.105 The situation is a little more complex if the carrier is partly at fault as well: thus, in an air context, perhaps the shipper cannot prove correct pre-transit cooling, but then the carrier cannot prove that it properly stored the cargo during a delay at a transhipment point.

9.106 In an ocean context, perhaps there is no proof of proper pre-cooling of the cargo, but the container arrives at the importer's pack-house direct from the discharge port with its vent closed. Both shipper and carrier are at fault.

9.107 In the past, the shipper's contributory negligence would have meant the Court would refuse to award any form of compensation, but presently, there is generally a more enlightened approach to the issue; if the parties cannot privately agree to share liability and adjust the amount of compensation accordingly, then a Court will determine the amount of fault on either side, and order compensation accordingly.

9.108 There will be some amplification of the above points in the following.

Pre-shipment causes

9.109 Unsurprisingly, this is an easy option for all carriers – both air and ocean – to put up as an objection.

9.110 You should have already provided the relevant export quality and pre-shipment cooling records, which on many occasions will prevent the carrier from raising any related objections, but it is not unknown for a carrier to simply dismiss them outright and imply incompetence on the part of the shipper.

9.111 This is, of course, ironic, because in many cases, the shipper (and grower if different from the shipper) will have been subjected to a detailed audit of its (or their) operations by a fully independent certification organisation representing the retailers supplied by them, before being permitted to supply product, whereas no carrier's operation is subjected to any such comparable audit.

9.112 For instance, in the face of photographs taken at the time of container loading showing temperature probes of the product, the carrier will still allege 'hot-stuffing' and be unimpressed when they are reminded of the evidence against that suggestion.

9.113 If you have a set of shelf-life tests relating to the specific consignment under claim, this obviously can be a powerful tool in negating the carrier's position.

9.114 Should your insistence that such records are completely reliable fail to persuade the carrier to yield, then you may have to consider instructing your solicitors.

9.115 Again, and to repeat: it is submitted that records of the product temperatures taken at the time of container loading, product inspection records, pictures of the container, the stowage, and the settings of the controls are sufficient in such circumstances.

9.116 The additional provision of shelf-life tests and records will strongly support your position.

Harvest records

9.117 It has not been entirely clear what has been meant by carriers when asking for this data and included in this has occasionally been seen the request for 'cutting' records.

9.118 It is not unreasonable for a carrier to require you to prove how long the product has spent between harvest and shipping, but it is not clear how a grower would specifically 'prove' the date on which it has 'cut' or harvested.

9.119 How would one document the harvesting and prove the link between the actual product and such a document? The answer seems not to have yet been found, and perhaps the grower can only assert how short a period there is between harvesting the product and its reaching the pack-house and being placed in a cold chamber to commence the removal of field heat.

Pack house protocols

9.120 Contrary to the period between harvest and arrival at the pack-house, once the product has reached the pack-house, it is presumed that the grower creates records to show its progress through (as applicable) sorting, washing, waxing, sizing, boxing up, palletising, and placement in the cool store.

9.121 Equally, the record of the pallet or carton being removed from the cool store for carriage to the airport or loading into the ocean container is presumed to be available.

'Hot stuffing' – ocean

9.122 In the context of ocean containers, it is not unusual for the carrier to allege that the product was loaded too warm.

9.123 Ideally, of course, the product should have been reduced in temperature to that which has been requested for carriage; handwritten records of checking temperature at the time of loading should counter this, but photos taken of temperature probes showing correct temperatures at the time of loading are normally definitive. Produce has been loaded at temperatures maybe 1 or 2°C above the requested carrying temperature, which carriers have alleged is the direct cause of loss, but which is almost certainly an untenable conclusion.

9.124 Further, if the thermograph(s) placed in the container by the shipper show more-or-less correct temperature from the beginning, this is good evidence of correct loading temperature. If the thermograph shows a strong and speedy 'pull-down' to more-or-less correct temperature immediately after loading, then this is also good evidence.

'Hot delivery' – air

9.125 In the context of air carriage, it is not so straightforward but easily dealt with.

9.126 If the product temperature has been proved at the time of departure of a consignment to the airport, and the journey is short, and perhaps a temperature-controlled vehicle has been used, the air carrier will have difficulty substantiating an allegation.

9.127 If the journey time is long, and no temperature-controlled vehicle is used, then an allegation of delivery to the airline too warm, thus pre-disposing the product to overheating during normal air carriage, will be difficult to disprove.

9.128 At the time of preparing this work, at least in Peru and in Jordan, it is known that the warehouse operators acting for various airlines issue a temperature document evidencing the temperature of cargo delivered to them, which eliminates any potential allegation of 'hot-loading'.

Mixed maturity

9.129 It is not uncommon for an ocean carrier to cite 'mixed maturity' of fruits or vegetables on out-turn as 'proof' that the products loaded by the shipper included a proportion of fruits or vegetables which were in an already advanced condition.

9.130 Consequently, this is regarded as a 'pre-shipment problem', but, in fact, it is a facile argument for carriers to use.

9.131 Whilst, of course, shippers can make mistakes, the frequency of a shipper loading product for a customer which was in such condition can only be extremely low.

9.132 The explanation, of course, is quite simple.

9.133 When harvesting fruits or vegetables, individual items are routinely selected for export within a narrow range of maturity to ensure they arrive with the customer in a still-unripe state or in an unadvanced condition.

9.134 However, being organic, each individual fruit or vegetable will mature at a very slightly different rate, and should temperature fail during transit, it is to be expected that some products will ripen and start to break down, while some will remain un-ripened or still in an unadvanced condition.

9.135 This has been seen by most people, when – for instance – they buy a half-dozen apples and leave them in the fruit bowl in the lounge. Days later, to find one apple developing a rot or forming mould on its surface does not mean that the supplier got it wrong.

9.136 Indeed, if and when temperature maintenance fails or a vent is inadvertently closed during transit, it would be miraculous if the fruits or vegetables were all at exactly the same stage of advancement or deterioration on out-turn.

9.137 Thus, 'mixed maturity' on out-turn is proof only of condition on out-turn, not of condition at the time of loading the container.

9.138 There always remains the possibility of faulty product selection by the shipper, but such a conclusion is not justified by citing 'mixed maturity' on out-turn, unless qualified or supported by other evidence, and production by the shipper of quality inspection records showing adherence to specific procedures becomes vital to refute such allegations.

9.139 Another observation to be made is that many shippers' selection processes are usually, in effect, a production line, where fruit is selected, graded, and packed for export. Product reaches the 'end of the line' and is usually or often palletised and cold stored, awaiting loading into a container or taken to the airport.

9.140 If 'mixed maturity' were 'evidence' of failure to select properly, then it is not logical or reasonable to suppose that one container or one air consignment of product alone could out-turn badly, when other containers or air consignments shipped around the same time do not, because product is surely never harvested as one discrete lot for one consignment.

Rots and diseases

9.141 A carrier's surveyor will report the presence of rots, and moulds, etc., if he or she observes them – he or she may opine that it is evidence of pre-shipment problems.

9.142 Whilst, again, shippers can make mistakes, it is a facile corollary for the surveyor to conclude this.

9.143 It is evident that during pre-shipment washing of fruit and some vegetables, it is simply not possible to eliminate all pathogens, and, consequently, product will go forward with some pathogens in their skins.

9.144 And, here, one of the fundamental purposes of reefer container carriage is demonstrated: if the reefer's refrigeration functions correctly, and stowage permits the cooled air to circulate as it should, those pathogens should be prevented from being sparked into life and multiplying with their attendant effects.

9.145 Of course, there are some pathogens which should have been eliminated in the nurturing of the products and which can cause problems during carriage – some moulds will thrive in cold conditions, and such moulds should have been prevented from being on the surface of the product.

9.146 Such particular pathogens should be well-known to the grower, in order for it to institute appropriate field management and, perhaps, a spray programme to eliminate them prior to export.

Thermographs

9.147 As referred to above, the placing of thermographs with consignments at the earliest possible opportunity cannot be emphasised enough: they will allow you to strongly refute allegations of hot stuffing and hot delivery.

Reefer container inspection

9.148 The conditions on the reverse of most carriers' bills of lading and waybills provide that shippers must inspect and satisfy themselves that the container is 'suitable' for carriage of their product.

9.149 Whilst this does not absolve a carrier from providing a properly ready container for a consignment, failure by a shipper to check all that it is able to inspect can result in its consignment out-turning at destination in a poor condition, and the carrier doing all possible to blame the shipper for the problems.

9.150 The carrier may not eventually succeed in blaming the shipper, but it certainly frustrates a claimant's efforts to obtain compensation.

9.151 A shipper must devise a container loading check sheet and keep it as a permanent record to be produced if necessary. The points to cover include:

- Temperature setting and reefer unit operation;
- Vent setting (although the vent can sometimes be obscured by a GenSet, of course, preventing it being checked);
- Cleanliness inside the container;
- Baffle plate in place;[10]
- Secure and air-tight door closure.

Vent closure and suffocation/CO_2 injury

9.152 As mentioned previously, unless the carrier's surveyor has concurred with the finding of such damage, provision of laboratory test results will enable this to be proven without difficulty; this should prevent any denial by the carrier.

Failures during transit

Inadequate packing

9.153 In general terms, it appears that inadequate packing is seldom encountered, but there are occasions when a shipper uses a carton which does not allow free circulation of air in the container, and, it has even been seen that a carton normally ideal for its purpose has been stacked on a pallet in such a way as to occlude ventilation holes.

9.154 Obviously, such fundamental problems must be avoided, and a shipper must be vigilant when considering any changes in its packaging supplier, or carton design.

Inadequate stowage in an ocean container

9.155 Stowage of your pallets or cartons must be done to ensure that there is free flow of cooled air.

9.156 Remember that in most reefer containers cooled air is forced through open channels in the floor, the principle being that the air will be forced upwards through the cartons or pallets to afford ventilation and to maintain product temperature.

10 A baffle plate is normally situated at the front of the container and its purpose is to ensure that the cooling air is properly directed into the various runnels which carry the air throughout the container.

9.157 Pallets have been known to collapse against each other, distorting the path of the circulating air, leading to 'pockets' of the cargo becoming warm causing advanced maturity during transit. A few fruits ripening at this time can trigger many other fruits into similar ripening, of course.

9.158 Hence, ensure that your pallets are not going to collapse, or become distorted.

Post-shipment objections

Attempts to reject claims on dis-entitlement

9.159 On rare occasions, a carrier may argue that a claimant is not entitled to pursue a claim, and thus, it is appropriate to be aware of which parties can pursue a claim.

9.160 In most cases, it is the consignee who is the party who sustains the loss and thus makes the claim.

9.161 Being in this position depends on two factors: one, the arrangements for the sale transaction between the shipper and consignee which can vary, and two, the generally unvarying assumption that when the consignee takes delivery of the consignment, the rights under the contract of carriage flow to the consignee.[11]

9.162 It follows, of course, that should a consignee refuse a consignment for any reason, the rights under the contract of carriage remain vested in the shipper; provided the reason for the refusal relates to a transit problem for which the carrier may be liable, the shipper is therefore entitled to pursue a claim against the carrier.

9.163 Any party properly authorised by the rightful claimant to act for them can pursue the matter, but in such a situation, it is appropriate for the party pursuing the claim to produce to the carrier a written authority from the actual claimant.

9.164 It can be agreed between the shipper and consignee that the shipper shall pursue the claim; this can be a voluntary agreement but will need to be proved to the carrier.

9.165 If the sale transaction is on a 'delivered at destination' basis,[12] or variation thereof, it necessarily follows that the shipper is rightfully entitled and likely to pursue the claim, since it is the shipper who has solely borne the risk of the shipment during the whole transit, and almost certainly retains ownership of the cargo.

9.166 On occasions, in the pursuit of economy, a shipper arranges the carriage through a forwarder, who acts as a (non-vessel or aircraft owning) carrier issuing its own contract of carriage, and separately contracts for the carriage with the carrier.

9.167 Forwarders who act in this manner can gather together several consignments, and 'consolidate' them into one consignment so far as the actual carrier is concerned, and it is this arrangement which can enable both shippers, and the forwarder, even so, to take advantage of the lower freight rates which apply to larger consignments.

9.168 There may be objections raised by airlines to dealing with claimants not named on the airline air waybill, and issues arising from this are dealt with above.[13]

---

11 Legal commentators will undoubtedly regard this as an over-simplified explanation, but it is intended for the general understanding of claimants who are not and do not need to be well-versed in the legal issues.

12 For additional information and more complete understanding regarding international sales transactions and the different arrangements which can be made and the implications thereof, readers should look into INCOTERMS which is readily accessible via the Internet.

13 See 'Air Cargo Consolidations and House Air Waybills' supra.

Air cargo

The grounds for a claim

9.169 Clearly, if a carrier loses a consignment during transit, there can be no defence which it can offer.

9.170 However, the majority of claims in our field appear to be based on damage caused by temperature abuse during transit.

9.171 With reference to the exposition of applicable air cargo law above,[14] there are interesting differences between the two versions of 'Warsaw' and 'Montreal'.

9.172 Warsaw permits the carrier a defence if it can prove that it did all that was reasonably necessary to safeguard the cargo, and despite those measures the cargo was still damaged. If it was impossible to take any such measures, then the carrier is similarly exonerated.

9.173 Montreal simply lays down that the carrier is liable for damage sustained in the event of destruction or loss of, or damage to cargo provided that the event which caused the damage was caused during air transportation[15] – clearly an entirely different approach to that in Warsaw.

9.174 In return for this 'blanket' assumed liability of the carrier, the carrier is entitled to defend itself by citing the following specific defences:[16]

1. Inherent defect, quality, or vice of the cargo;
2. Defective packing;
3. An act of war or an armed conflict;
4. An act of public authority carried out in connection with the entry, exit, or transit of the cargo.

9.175 The third defence is exceedingly rare, of course, but if it should arise, there is likely to be little doubt of it!

9.176 The fourth defence is, again, seldom encountered, but clearly has to do with irregularities on the consignment falling outside of the carrier's remit – nevertheless, if the consignment is delayed in some way, but is still in the care of the carrier and supposing the irregularities are resolved and the cargo released by the authority, the carrier's duty of care has remained in force, and it must have done all possible to safeguard the consignment during the time.

9.177 If it has not, then there is a *prima facie* case against the carrier even so.

Force majeure issues

9.178 Sometimes a carrier will advise that the damage has occurred outside of its control and that accordingly they cannot be held responsible for it.

9.179 This is not a proper defence and if a claimant is not satisfied with it, it is entitled to question it because both Warsaw and Montreal specify how a carrier can defend itself.

14 See 'An Overview of the Legal Framework for Air Cargo' supra.

15 As defined in Article 2 – but for general understanding, it is effectively whilst the cargo is in the possession of the carrier. However, if there is transportation 'outside of an airport' in connection with carriage of the cargo, this can still be regarded as 'air transportation' in the possession of the carrier.

16 Article 18.2.

9.180 As above, in Warsaw, it must prove that it took all necessary measures, etc., and in Montreal, it is limited to specific defences.

9.181 However, there are interesting questions within Montreal in regard to what constitutes an 'event': at first sight, it appears that anything which happens is an 'event'. However, it is submitted that the event must relate to the carrier's handling of the cargo in some relevant way, but the writer is currently unaware of any legal precedents so far in regard to the meaning of the word in this context.

Successive carriage

9.182 For the claimant, this point is more to do with the practicality of pursuing a claim than anything else.

9.183 Successive carriage occurs where an air waybill is made out showing the first sector of the carriage to be carried out by one airline, and for another airline to complete the second part of the carriage.

9.184 This enables the consignee in his own country to submit the claim to the second carrier and hold the second carrier liable even though the first carrier may have been the carrier at fault. In other words, the second carrier stands in the place of the first in regard to liability for the loss. The converse is, of course, true for the shipper.

9.185 A problem arises where a forwarder acting for a shipper arranges carriage with one airline subject to an air waybill to a transhipment point, and separately arranges with a second airline for carriage to the final destination, and that carriage is subject to a separate air waybill.

9.186 This is not as uncommon as one may suppose, and the motive in making this arrangement is, of course, to save money on freight charges – laudable, of course – but self-defeating if the first carrier is the one at fault, and the second carrier can exonerate itself. From a pure claims point of view, it is the equivalent of 'shooting oneself in the foot'.

9.187 With no grounds to litigate against the second carrier, submitting a claim in a country other than one's own brings with it its own problems; the carrier may be able to ignore the claim with impunity because the claimant may find the prospect of litigating in a country other than its own a seriously daunting prospect.

USA head-quartered airlines and the 'three-day rule'

9.188 This issue regularly surfaces with several of these airlines, on the premise that a consignment must be packed sufficiently well to withstand a three-day transit.

9.189 If the carriage of a consignment has been completed within a period of three days but out-turns at destination with temperature abuse-type damage, it is usual to receive a message advising that the airline cannot be held responsible for any damage, on the premise that it could not have been packed properly.

9.190 Such a defence is seriously flawed in relation to both Warsaw and Montreal provisions as stated above – effectively, it is not a defence – but that does not stop it being used; in the majority of cases, issuing a protest and pointing out the error of their ways results in a long period of silence from the respondents, unrelieved by repeated chasers.

9.191 However, in the writer's experience, on every occasion that their position has been challenged through instructed lawyers, these airlines concede and settle; however, it is unfortunate that it has almost always taken a perceived threat of litigation to force them to concede.

9.192 Of course, it is undoubted that with proper and diligent handling by the airline, practically all perishables consignments are packed to withstand three days' carriage!

9.193 A case decided in the Florida Court in 2007[17] would appear to make it clear that US-based airlines cannot succeed with this defence. Although the Court did not specifically refer to the '3-day rule', it found that the airline concerned had neglected to advise the consignee for 18 hours whilst the asparagus consignment sat in the hot sun, and that this was the cause of the damage, which rather suggests that the 3-day rule is a 'non-point' in relation to the applicable law in the eyes of the Court.

Limitation of liability

9.194 The principle behind the limiting of carrier's liability is that it is recompense to carriers as result of laying down only specific methods of avoiding liability, leaving other avenues for defending unavailable to them.

9.195 Fortunately, there are few perishables consignments which are affected by these provisions since their value does not exceed the carrier's maximum liability limitation.

9.196 The only examples known to the writer are valuable herbs – think of saffron – which are exceptionally light in relation to their value, and vanilla pods of which the value can be extraordinarily high.

9.197 Whilst the original wordings of both the Warsaw and Montreal conventions do not read thus, there has been enlightened legislation in many countries permitting a value of 22[18] SDRs[19] per kilogram to be applied as the limitation, which represents a modest increase from the original.

9.198 Thus, and as an illustration in respect of the UK, on a 10 kg carton a carrier cannot be made to pay more than 10 kg × 22 × GBP 0.9788[20] = GBP 215.34. There are few perishable commodities which would be valued for retail at over GBP 21.53 per kg at the period during which this has been set down.

Enforcement of these rules

9.199 Article 23 of Warsaw and Article 26 of Montreal provide that a carrier cannot reduce its liability below that set down within Warsaw and Montreal.

9.200 As these treaties form part of the law of States which adhere to them, carriers can neither find grounds for rejection of claims other than provided within those treaties, nor can they settle for less than their limited liability or the claimed amount,[21] whichever is the smaller.

9.201 On the secondary point, however, it is commonly found that a carrier will offer less than they should, and a claimant will often accept such an offer in order to conclude the matter, and 'move on'. This point will be explored in more detail in 'Settlements' below.

Ocean cargo

Attempts to reject claims on dis-entitlement

9.202 Much of what is shown above in regard to air claims applies to ocean cargo.

17 Wea Farms v American Airlines [S.D. Fla Apr. 18, 2007].
18 At the time of writing.
19 See above in Definitions.
20 The value of the SDR on the day of setting down this calculation.
21 Provided, of course, it is calculated in accordance with the laws applicable.

9.203 Thus, should there be a forwarders' bill of lading or sea waybill, it should not be difficult to have the forwarder issue a cession of rights in favour of the rightful claimant, which should be persuasive in having the carrier deal with the claim.

9.204 There is some variation between jurisdictions should it become necessary to move onto litigation, but at such a point, a claimant will be taking advice from a lawyer, in any case.

The grounds for the claim

9.205 Contrary to the provisions within the air cargo rules, those for ocean carriage are more complex.

9.206 In each Article IV of both Hague and Hague/Visby, there is laid down an extensive list of possible defences which the carrier is permitted to use. Thus, the carrier cannot be held responsible for loss or damage in the following situations:

- The carrier is not responsible for unseaworthiness unless they have failed to act with due diligence. This applies to holds, refrigeration facilities, and properly crewing the vessel;
- Act, neglect, or fault by the crew or a pilot in the navigation of the vessel;
- Fire, unless caused by actual fault of the carrier;
- Perils, dangers, and accident of the sea;
- Act of god;
- Act of war;
- Act of public enemies;
- Arrest or restraint of princes, rulers, or people, or seizure under legal process;
- Quarantine restrictions;
- Strikes or lockouts or restraint of labour;
- Riots and civil commotions;
- Saving or attempting to save life or property at sea;
- Wastage arising from inherent defect, quality, or vice of the goods;
- Insufficiency of packing;
- Latent defects not discoverable by due diligence;
- Any other cause arising without the actual fault or privity of the carriage.

9.207 The wording of some of these points has been shortened or simplified for this work, and if any of them should be used by a carrier in its defence, and the claimant has difficulty in either understanding or accepting them, then referral to the full wording should be made, of course.

9.208 The exact and precise meaning of the various points has exercised carriers and claimants for many years in their attempts to succeed in their arguments, and hence a large body of law has arisen from the Courts interpreting these wordings.

9.209 If, as would seem likely, the claimant continues to be dissatisfied with the carrier's rejection despite reviewing the full wording, it is probably the occasion for seeking a marine lawyer's guidance.

9.210 Finally, it should be borne in mind that the carrier must reasonably prove that it is entitled to use these defences; it cannot claim relief from them without reasonable evidence.

Shipper's responsibility for container settings

9.211 In the section above, entitled 'Reefer container inspection', it is explained that carrier's bills of lading or sea waybill routinely have a clause in them placing responsibility on the shipper for checking that container settings are correct when they load containers.

9.212 There is a question of how much responsibility the shipper should reasonably be expected to have in this regard.

9.213 Irrespective of any other consideration, it appears to be a world-wide arrangement that carriers do not allow shippers to set container controls.

9.214 Clearly, it is entirely within the shipper's interest to check out settings at the time of loading, but on the other hand, the carrier effectively has two opportunities to verify that the settings are correct; firstly, when the container is released to the shipper, obviously the controls must be set in accordance with the request made by the shipper, and secondly, when the loaded container is received back into the port ready for loading on board the vessel.

9.215 The only correct actions for the shipper at this stage of the carriage must be to confirm the settings at the time of loading, and to immediately bring to the attention of the carrier any incorrect setting, with the exception of the vent if it is obscured by the GenSet.

9.216 Following that, the shipper must make sure that the carrier re-adjusts the settings. On rare occasions, it is known for the carrier to instruct the shipper how to make the adjustment, and if this should happen, then it is strongly advised that the event be documented appropriately with a written record, even quoting the name of the carrier staff-member giving the instructions.

9.217 If the survey at out-turn reports that the container was incorrectly set, it can lead to serious disputes between the claimant and the carrier, if the shipper has not checked the setting when loading, which at worst can prevent a claim being settled, or result in a much-compromised settlement well below the level of losses sustained. If the shipper was unable to check the setting, then the carrier cannot resort to blaming the shipper, of course, which is particularly relevant in the case of a gen-set obscuring the vent.

Inadequate stowage

9.218 It is the nature of our business that – in general terms – problems with fresh produce tend to be noticed when the cargo is unloaded from the container at the receiver's pack-house, and, on many occasions, not until the receiver carries out a quality inspection.

9.219 Of course, it would be ideal on every occasion if the receiver could remove a couple of pallets and check quality before the bulk of the load is removed from the container, thus enabling them to determine if there is a problem (but it is accepted that this is seldom practical).

9.220 Thus, the correctness of stowage can be checked to see if air circulation has been disrupted, allowing uneven cooling of parts of the cargo to occur, but, of course, in the majority of cases, the cargo is unloaded by handlers who are not necessarily alert to stowage problems.

9.221 If the thermograph placed in the container by the shipper reveals temperature problems, but the carrier's datalogger shows a steady supply of air at the correct temperature and an air return temperature raised, the carrier will almost always suspect poor stowage, and allege that such is the cause of the problem.

9.222 It is then difficult for the claimant to deny that this was the case because stowage has not been checked on out-turn.

9.223 Hence, shippers and importers should ensure that stowage is correct on out-turn: if you are not doing this, then you should make the point of including it in your procedures and ensure that those who unload your containers are alert to the problem, and report that there was no such problem or that there was.

9.224 If there was a problem, then, of course, it can be dealt with for the future by liaison between importers and shippers, and similar such problems avoided in the future.

Carrier's datalogger – if it can be obtained

9.225 It is, of course, vital for claimants whose claims are rejected on the grounds that the carrier's datalogger shows that there was no problem with temperature control within the container to obtain and study the carrier's datalogger but obtaining those dataloggers is routinely difficult.

9.226 A minority of carriers will produce their data on request, but most carriers, including 'household' names, when requested to provide proof of their position, often react with silence, and on occasion, a straight refusal.

9.227 One might suppose that if the datalogger proves the carrier's position, they would release it without delay, but, since they do not, it is difficult to avoid a claimant supposing that they have something to hide and are not being truthful.

9.228 It engenders distrust, and the only way to force this evidence into the open may be to litigate and progress the proceedings, by which time, the claimant will have incurred significant costs, and still not have a real feeling as to whether its efforts will result in success.

9.229 Even when the datalogger is produced for inspection by the claimant, there are various versions, and some are extremely difficult to read, filled with immense amounts of data, confusing, and intimidating.

9.230 This often makes it necessary to secure the services of a reefer expert to interpret the data and try to reconcile it with the shipper's thermogram.

Malfunctioning containers and 'due diligence'

9.231 Article 4.2 and 4.2.(p) in both the Hague and Hague/Visby Rules, reads thus:

> Neither the Carrier nor the Ship shall be responsible for loss or damage arising or resulting from:
>
> Latent defects not discoverable by due diligence.

9.232 Clearly, in the current context, such matters involve breakdown or faulty performance of the reefer unit, and one can expect the carrier to attempt to show that the container had been properly prepared for transit before release to the shipper.

9.233 Whilst this does appear entirely unfair to claimants, allowing carriers to escape liability, it does reflect what is generally the case in society, that a party cannot be held responsible in a claim unless it can be shown that they were negligent in some way. (Expert legal opinion would undoubtedly consider this an over-simplification of the principle involved.)

9.234 The carrier must explain what the fault was, and why and how it could not be detected prior to release of the container to the shipper. The carrier should produce a 'pre-trip inspection' report, and careful examination of it should be carried out against the known fault.

9.235 After all, a diligently maintained road vehicle very seldom suffers a breakdown, and a reefer unit is clearly a less complex piece of machinery than a car, and, so, a claimant is entitled to be rightly sceptical about evidence produced by a carrier in this situation.

Measure of damages

9.236 In the special case of the 'supermarket market' in the UK referred to above, carriers may insist that the wholesale market is the only market they should be considering and have generally refused to discuss the issues. (However, bear in mind those very few jurisdictions which link quantum to export invoice prices.)

9.237 When claimants have instructed their legal and other representatives to insist on the correct values, the reaction has been either to simply confirm the previous offer without comment, or possibly slightly raise the offer, supposing that the claimant will be tempted by it rather than continue to press for more at an indeterminate date in the future.

9.238 When the point has been pressed further by claimants, such has been met with outright hostility, and assertions that claimants will have to go to trial with strict evidence – a prospect which is both daunting and *prima facie* a worthless financial exercise for the claimant, who could well expect to find itself with a significant bill for costs since such costs cannot be expected to be fully recovered in the English Court.

9.239 The point appears to strongly meet the requirements of foreseeability,[22] since the existence of the different markets cannot be denied, and the point has been brought repeatedly to the carriers' attention for over 30 years by and to the writer's knowledge.

9.240 In this context, there appears to be no practical way in which claimants can actually obtain the compensation to which they are truly entitled, until and unless one of them decides to accept that it must pay for the principle involved, and, since all such businesses are financial exercises, this seems unlikely.

9.241 The writer has not encountered a similar situation in other States, but presumably it similarly exists elsewhere.

9.242 In various States, other than the UK, the wholesale market is the main supplier of produce to retailers, and thus, there is not the same problem, since reports of prevailing prices can be easily obtained, and the carrier is not in a position to dismiss them.

9.243 Turning to the Hague and Hague/Visby Rules, there are differences in this context: Hague does not lay down any definition of the measure of damages, whereas Hague/Visby states the following in Article 4.5(b):

> The total amount recoverable shall be calculated by reference to the value of such goods at the place and time at which the goods are discharged from the ship in accordance with the contract or should have been so discharged.
>
> The value of the goods shall be fixed according to the commodity exchange price, or, if there be no such price, according to the current market price, or, if there be no commodity exchange price or current market price, by reference to the normal value of goods of the same kind and quality.

9.244 Two points arise from this.

9.245 Firstly, there are some jurisdictions in which it is argued that because Hague has no formula for measure of damages, other rules should be applied.

22 See supra – paragraphs 6.13–6.28, and 9.80

9.246 Some few jurisdictions look at the supply invoice value, but in most of both civil law and common law jurisdictions, the rules on measure of damages are broadly similar.

9.247 For instance, in France, Article 1150 of the Civil Code, which is difficult to misinterpret, is not really different from the rules established under English common law in the case of Hadley v Baxendale,[23] in which, incidentally, French civil law was cited.

9.248 It is understood that these rules are broadly similar in many jurisdictions, and so, it appears that carriers cannot derogate from them – if they do so by offering less than the correctly calculated quantum, then claimants should strongly challenge them, and seek the proper amount.

9.249 If the difference in the offer and quantum is significant, it may be justified to make and follow through with the threat of legal action.

9.250 The second point concerns the special situation in the UK in regard to the 'supermarket market' issue – in the last line of the above Hague/Visby definition, 'by reference to the normal value of goods of the same kind and quality', it seems that it is not so difficult for supermarket suppliers or importers to succeed in establishing that they can obtain similar products only from similar suppliers and certified growers and shipper, and not at all from the wholesale market.

9.251 This argument would appear to be 'water-tight', but still may well not succeed in persuading carriers to settle in accordance with properly calculated quantum.

Limitation of liability

9.252 Limitation appears to be an uncommon problem so far as perishable produce is concerned in ocean carriage.

9.253 Nonetheless, it is worth having an outline of how this works in the ocean carriage context in case your cargo has an exceptional value.

9.254 We encounter limitation in the Hague Rules Article 4.5 in the guise of a package limitation of £100[24] – the Hague Rules were agreed in 1924, and the £100 is now generally regarded as the modern value of £100 gold in 1924 (certainly under English law). Hence, limitation is most unlikely to be a factor in perishables claims falling under these rules.

9.255 Secondly, we encounter limitation in the Hague/Visby Rules as 2 SDRs per kilo, or 666.67 SDRs per package,[25] whichever if the higher. Thus, in general terms, we encounter limitation at 2 SDRs per kg, which calculates to 2 × GBP 0.9788[26] = GBP 1.98 per kg.

9.256 Few fresh produce commodities moved by sea appear to exceed this value, with the exceptions known to the writer of spring onions,[27] flowers, and decorative foliage. Doubtless there are other commodities, of course.

9.257 Vanilla pods and saffron are clearly exceptionally valuable, of course, but it is not known to the writer if such are moved by sea.

---

23 Hadley v Baxendale (1854) 9 Ex 341. Under the first 'limb' of this case, losses are recoverable where they flow directly from the breach of contract. Under the second 'limb', indirect losses are recoverable where those losses would have been within the reasonable contemplation of the parties when they entered into the contract.

24 Article 4(5).

25 Article 4(5) of Hague as amended by the Brussels Protocol of 1968, and a second protocol in 1979.

26 The value of the SDR on the day of setting down this calculation.

27 Known variously as scallions and green onions.

9.258 If your consignment is of a commodity exceeding the value of GBP 1.98 per kg arrived-sound market value (or your currency equivalent thereof), there is little that can be done about it.

9.259 To learn that you cannot succeed in recovering the full value of your consignment, owing to the limitation rules, can be quite a shock, and if you are contemplating moving highly valuable products, transit insurance cover is clearly a positive consideration.

Unreasonable attitudes and commercial 'strong-arm' tactics

9.260 This section of this work contains iterations of points made elsewhere, but it does effectively summarise many of the forms of resistance that a claimant can encounter.

9.261 From time to time, attitudes on the part of carriers' claims handlers are extremely difficult to understand.

9.262 Some claims handlers are amicable, and even when rejecting a claim, they are courteous and explain clearly, and when their position is disputed, they remain both courteous and professional.

9.263 Others, sadly, exhibit some extraordinary reactions and one is left to wonder why they appear to treat their customers[28] almost as enemies, throwing doubt on their competence in the work in which they specialise, and dismissing clear evidence without comment.

Field-heat argument

9.264 The carrier alleges 'hot' loading followed by a patronising statement informing a claimant that containers are not to be used to remove field heat.

9.265 Such allegations appear to be made despite, for instance, that the shipper has been successfully exporting the product in excess of 20 years, and extensively using the carrier making the allegation.

9.266 The claimant may have a sound reputation for its product's quality, as a result of repeated 'audits' of all aspects of their operations by unimpeachable certifying organisations, and a long record of its product being routinely received in sound condition at destination.

Improper use of authorities

9.267 Some claims handlers affect a didactic and patronising approach to long and highly experienced exporters and importers and cite their alleged incompetence on superficial knowledge gleaned from authoritative texts.

9.268 Also such data can be taken out of context and thus used incorrectly, and no amount of refutation on the part of the claimant will 'shake' the claims handler out of his or her misconception.

28 As above, a consignee/importer/claimant is in effect also the customer of the carrier, despite the shipper being the party which concluded the contract of carriage, since consignees have much influence on which carriers are preferred and which are to be avoided by the shipper.

'Strong-arm tactics'

9.269 There have been threats to embargo shippers. Fortunately, this is exceedingly rare, but continues to remain a possibility. The writer has experienced this in relation to his clients' claims on several occasions – fortunately, none in recent years – and, in particular, on one occasion, when the client was actually giving evidence in a trial. Both the client and the shipper buckled under the pressure: the claim was withdrawn, and they were even forced to pay the carrier's legal costs.

9.270 Shippers and importers know that there are some countries from which airlines are able to provide less than sufficient capacity, and so it is a matter of survival for a shipper to obtain enough space to make its export business viable, and for the importer to ensure the more-or-less free flow of product.

9.271 A threat by an airline to embargo a shipper's product is difficult for a shipper and its customer to resist, and what choice do exporters and importers have but to buckle under this pressure and absorb losses which rightfully should be compensated?

9.272 Nonetheless, this is a fact of commerce, and if it happens to you, it becomes a matter of whether you are in a strong-enough position to see the claim through, or whether you must swallow your sense of injustice in the pursuit of survival.

Refusal to produce evidence

9.273 It is not unusual for carriers, particularly ocean carriers, to demand every piece of evidence from claimants, whilst refusing to produce their own.

9.274 Of course, it is necessary to bear in mind that there are clear duties on the claimant to produce evidence to prove its claim, but equally there are clear duties on the respondent carrier to produce evidence to back up its assertions.

9.275 The problem is, of course, that the only way to compel carriers to produce, for instance, their dataloggers to prove their reefer operated without problem, is to litigate or make a clear and credible threat of litigation.

9.276 In this regard, the carrier's grounds for refusal are often along the lines of 'it is not our policy to release datalogger records to third parties'.

9.277 Such an attitude is beyond comprehension, since if this data does support the carriers' claims rejections, claimants will probably desist from efforts to obtain settlement.

Being 'taken to the wire'

9.278 You may not be able to get a substantive response, only a series of holding replies, and it is not unusual for major law firms who accept instructions from claimants to face this as well.

9.279 With air claims there is a two-year period allowed for the settlement of a claim, in the absence of which a claimant has no choice but to issue Court proceedings; since air claims are subject to a two-year time-bar period, it seems more difficult for an airline to delay concluding with the claimant beyond this period.

9.280 However, with ocean carriers, the situation is different: a one-year period is allowed, at the expiry of which, an extension can be agreed between carrier and claimant; however, what happens when the absence of negotiation comes up against the time bar, and the carrier refuses to grant an extension, or simply does not respond to a claimant's request for an extension?

9.281 The claimant is faced with an invidious decision on whether to risk commencing Court proceedings with the attendant costs and expose itself to the risk of having to pay the carrier's costs.

9.282 Who could doubt that this is well-known to carriers, such that some claims simply 'fall away'?

Further carrier tactics after issue of proceedings

9.283 Many carriers choose, for instance, English jurisdiction in their terms and conditions, despite their being domiciled in another State.

9.284 Hitherto you will have had to deal with claims handlers employed by a company, being a subsidiary of the carrier, incorporated in the country in which you make the claim.

9.285 In the event that negotiations break down, or more usually it seems, do not get started, Court proceedings are issued but cannot be served on the 'local company', because it is not the actual carrier, and your solicitors' request to be advised of local solicitors who will accept service on behalf of the carrier is met with silence.

9.286 You are then left with a further unenviable decision as to whether to serve outside the jurisdiction on the carrier in its home location; you must conform to the laws of that country, and costs spiral upwards with translations, appointment of solicitors in that country, etc.

9.287 Additionally, you again cannot overlook the exposure to having to pay the carrier's costs if you are unsuccessful in your claim.

9.288 Again, who could doubt that this is well-known to carriers, resulting in claims simply 'falling away'?

Dismissal of evidence

9.289 Following carrier's demands for pre-shipment temperature and export condition proofs, they are seemingly ignored or met with a response such as a declaration that despite that evidence their own data proves 'hot-loading' (but, as above, they fail to provide that evidence).

9.290 There have been instances where the provision of the shipper's shelf-life tests of product taken from the relevant shipment which has out-turned badly, proving that the product could well withstand the transit, has also been effectively dismissed by the carrier.

9.291 It is understood, for instance, that where shippers are certified for supply to British supermarkets, the recording of all the above evidence is a requirement for their certification.

Excessive demands for evidence

9.292 Over recent years, carriers – and, particularly, ocean carriers – have required increasing amounts of evidence from claimants: intricate details of harvesting, selection, cooling, timing, and so on.

9.293 Allegations, both implicit and explicit, are made of incompetent preparation by shippers of consignments – this, despite the claims handlers purporting to be qualified to interpret those pre-shipment records with undoubtedly inferior knowledge of the subject.

9.294 And these extensive requirements are expressed even when there is ample evidence of, for instance, temperature abuse during transit – either chill or heating – or CO_2 injury.

9.295 Thus, a carrier will take up a position where it is preparing to allege, or indeed alleges, inherent vice or 'hot-loading'.

9.296 It is difficult for claimants to avoid concluding that such demands are made only with the express intention of over-burdening claimants with provision of proofs to intimidate them into 'falling away'.

9.297 These matters concern the burden of proof, referred to elsewhere in this book, but to iterate the point, if it is established that cargo is shipped in apparent good condition but is discharged damaged, the burden of proof is on the carrier to prove that it did not breach its obligation to take reasonable care.

9.298 Additionally, where the carrier has shown that there may be an exception to liability as provided for within the applicable rules, it is not for the claimant to disprove this, but for the carrier to prove it.

9.299 Of course, in the early days of a claim, it is evidently worthwhile for a claimant to go to the trouble of obtaining all this evidence from its supplier, in the pursuit of persuading the carrier that it must settle the claim to obviate, if possible, the carrier alleging pre-shipment problems.

9.300 It is also worthwhile on occasion, it seems, to obtain the shipper's laid-down procedures for the preparation of export consignments, since, if the claim 'goes legal', such evidence can only bolster other evidence.

Mixed maturity

9.301 This point is also expanded elsewhere.

9.302 The carrier's surveyor alleges that mixed maturity on out-turn is evidence of failure to select properly by the exporter, when it can only be evidence of condition on out-turn.

9.303 Such a stance was maintained in the face of production of certificated shipper procedures and evidence of multiple consignments from that shipper of over 30 years' standing, who operates a production line, and at that time had no other consignment outturning at destination in a similar condition.

Carrier's claims, operational, and marketing personnel at odds?

9.304 The writer has interviewed operations and marketing personnel of different carriers at load ports who pronounced themselves entirely satisfied with a shipper's preparation of consignments, only to find their own claims department allege incompetence on the part of the shipper, with the customary 'hot' loading, improper stowage, mixed maturity, or inadequate packaging having been cited.

9.305 It is presumably naïve to suppose that the hitherto-satisfied operations and marketing personnel would be prepared to stand against their own company in support of a customer's claim, except, perhaps, where the claimant is a source of particularly high revenue to the company.

CHAPTER 10

Reaching for settlements

Without prejudice negotiations

10.1 Firstly, a few comments regarding the term 'without prejudice' – widely used and widely misunderstood – are appropriate.

10.2 The true purpose and value of 'without prejudice' exchanges is to cover the discussions (and any associated correspondence) between the parties with legal privilege, meaning that the parties can feel free to discuss settlement without fear of that discussion being put before a judge or arbitrator if negotiations break down.

10.3 Few exporters and importers have legal training, and they may be puzzled by routinely encountering the expression in carriers' communications, and if they deal with lawyers or insurers acting for carriers.

10.4 It appears to be greatly overused by claims handlers and appears to be pointless in many circumstances.

10.5 When used by claims handlers, it appears they are trying to guard against anything they set down in communications being used against them – this, at the same time as rejecting a potential claim at first instance, when acknowledging a notice of claim.

10.6 The term is applied to many of their communications, but it is most unlikely that they can establish 'privilege' for any of these documents; privilege is the legal principle that any document prepared in contemplation of legal action – for instance, a lawyer's advice to a client, or an expert's opinion commissioned by a legal representative of the client – may be withheld and not produced to the opposing claimant or plaintiff or their representatives.

10.7 If the carrier communicates and releases documents or data to the claimant, there can have been no point in describing any such data as 'without prejudice'. It is clearly 'evidence' and cannot properly be withheld in the event of litigation.

10.8 The term becomes of importance when negotiations commence, if they do: during negotiations neither party wishes to be bound by anything said or written before their final decisions are taken, which seems fair enough.

10.9 Accordingly, it is appropriate to state in negotiation-communications that all such are 'without prejudice'; it would, of course, be more accurate to state 'without prejudice to our (or our client's) final decision in this matter'.

10.10 On the other hand, such a statement applied to other communications not falling within a negotiation context appears to be largely meaningless.

10.11 Turning to actual negotiations, there appears to be no definitive textbook to follow.

DOI: 10.4324/9781003219231-10

10.12 Negotiation skills can certainly be acquired but perhaps never actually perfected, but can they be applied to a situation where one party is simply trying to persuade another to pay as much of their claim as possible, and the other is attempting to pay as little as possible?

10.13 Each side will have its arguments, and they will be persuasive or not – seldom in our context do the parties meet and lay out their positions and discuss them, and it is even less likely that claimants will be present at any meetings which may take place between legal representatives where very substantial claims are concerned.

10.14 Experience appears to show that there is a 'tipping point' between disputants – it may be determined through various means. Either side may have a target amount in mind which it will agree to in order to bring an end to the matter.

10.15 Claimants tend to be influenced by being 'out-of-pocket' for a long period and may be approaching a point of desperation to obtain any settlement to maintain their viability. Additionally, claimants may have incurred substantial legal costs which are damaging their profits or are equally threatening their viability also.

10.16 Larger exporters and importers can finance the sometimes-long waiting-periods and legal costs, although any financial director 'worth his salt' is going to keep a withering gaze on costs, of course, keeping in mind that any such project must be reduced to a financial exercise at the end of the day.

10.17 There seems little room for 'principle' in these matters.

10.18 Carriers are not so constrained: for them it is a simple exercise in avoiding settlements or reducing them to the absolute minimum. Most claims handlers probably report – in the final analysis – to the finance division of their company, which 'protects' them from the marketing division which will often want claims settled so that they can enjoy optimum relations with the customer who has suffered a loss.

Dispute resolution

10.19 Alternative Dispute Resolution (ADR) offers a route to resolving disputes between claimants and carriers which do not involve litigation.

10.20 Governments tend to want to encourage the development of ADR, since it holds out the prospect of reducing the State's costs in maintaining the legal 'machine'.

10.21 Forms of ADR which would seem to hold out benefit in our context are:

- MEDIATION: in which an independent third party helps the disputing parties to come to a mutually acceptable outcome;
- EARLY NEUTRAL EVALUATION, where an independent third party considers the facts and takes a decision often binding on one or both parties.

10.22 Sadly, ADR seems to be almost unheard of in our commercial sector, which seems unfortunate, despite it having been introduced into the UK Civil Procedural Rules[1] in 2015.

1 Rule 3.1(2)(m).

10.23 A more formal means of dispute resolution is 'arbitration': bills of lading and sea waybills often include in the carrier's conditions shown on the reverse an 'arbitration clause', but the way in which these clauses are drafted tends unfortunately to lead to very significant and potentially disproportionate costs in the context of the category of cargo claims contemplated in this book.

10.24 Accordingly, one would suppose that mediation or early neutral evaluation should be sought by both claimants and carriers in our commercial sector, and it is to be hoped that this will happen in due course.

Ocean carriers' P&I clubs

10.25 From time to time, carriers may refer to their 'Club', or their 'P&I club', which may become more-or-less involved in a claim, and it is not unusual, even, for a 'Club' to communicate and negotiate direct on behalf of its 'member'.

10.26 For claimants it signals little difference in regard to the way in which respondents – whoever they may be – conduct the claim, except, perhaps, that communications can be considerably lengthened, and progress significantly slowed down.

10.27 Whilst it makes little difference to the claimant, it is probably worth having a general understanding of what is involved.

10.28 'Protection and indemnity insurance' is a form of maritime liability insurance provided by a P&I club.

10.29 A marine insurance company provides 'hull and machinery' cover for shipowners, and cargo cover for cargo owners, but a P&I club provides cover for a carrier's third-party risks for damage caused to cargo during carriage, war risks, and risks of environmental damage such as oil spills and pollution.

10.30 In the UK, both traditional underwriters and P&I clubs are subject to the Marine Insurance Act 1906.

10.31 A P&I club is a mutual insurance association that provides risk pooling, information, and representation for its members.

10.32 Unlike a marine insurance company, which reports to its shareholders, a P&I club reports only to its members. Originally, P&I club members were typically shipowners, ship operators, or demise charterers, but more recently freight forwarders and warehouse operators have been able to join.

10.33 Whereas an insured party pays a premium to an underwriter for cover which lasts for a particular time (say, a year, or a voyage), a P&I club member instead pays a 'call', which is a sum of money that is put into the Club's pool – a fund for the 'benefit' of all members.

10.34 If, at the end of the year, there are still funds in the pool, each member will pay a reduced call the following year; but if, for example, the Club has dealt with an environmental claim following an oil spillage, Club members will immediately have to pay a further call to replenish the pool.

Jurisdiction

10.35 It is inevitable that some claims cannot be resolved by compromise, if the claimant strongly believes in the merits of its claim, and the carrier either does not, or simply refuses to respond.

10.36 Thus, the claimant has little choice other than to instruct lawyers to act for it.

10.37 Thus, there are various points that are worth a claimant knowing, so that it can have an understanding of what must happen, and thus, here is an attempt to demystify this daunting prospect to some degree.

Air

10.38 The general rule in air cargo cases which may be subject to litigation is that a claimant can only sue a carrier in specific jurisdictions.

10.39 The jurisdiction is determined as the place in which the shipment was delivered into the carrier's possession for carriage by air,[2] the place of destination where the air carriage terminated, or the place where the contract of carriage was concluded.

10.40 Here follow some examples to illustrate the points.

- If the carrier has agreed to collect, and truck from one country to another, as, for instance, a collection in Gambia but load on board the aircraft in Senegal, the place of jurisdiction is Senegal. Of course, this particular instance would be of relevance only to the shipper;
- Conversely, if a consignment is unloaded from the aircraft in the Netherlands and trucked to the UK on the air carrier's trucking service, the place of jurisdiction should, at first sight, be the Netherlands, although, on the reverse of a standard IATA resolution 600b air waybill is a clause stating that the carrier has the opportunity to insert other conditions if it so desires; this suggests that whilst such trucking is subject to CMR[3] rules, it could be that the carrier in the absence of a declaration or insertion of such rules is content to be subject only to air carriage rules;
- Occasionally, an air carriage contract is concluded in one country but relates to carriage of cargo between two other countries. In such a case, a claimant can bring a legal action in the first country.

10.41 Before air carriage was properly regulated internationally, it was possible for a claimant to take legal action in a jurisdiction which gave him the greatest advantage. This was called 'forum shopping' and could greatly disadvantage a carrier.

10.42 With Warsaw and Montreal treaties this is no longer possible, of course.

---

2 Meaning that if a carrier should take charge of a consignment in one country and truck it to another where the actual air carriage begins, jurisdiction can only be in the country where the air carriage began.

3 CMR, Contrat pour la Merchandise par Route – the international treaty covering transport by road which is the law of most countries in Europe and extends into the Middle East.

Ocean

10.43 Neither Hague nor Hague/Visby sets down any provision regarding where a claimant can take legal action, which has left carriers free to specify the jurisdiction in which they can be sued.

10.44 The chosen jurisdiction is specified in a condition on the reverse of the bill of lading or waybill.

10.45 Clearly, this can be very inequitable for a claimant.

10.46 As an example, if a shipper in South America or a consignee in Europe suffers a loss on a Japanese carrier, there may be no choice other than to litigate in the Japanese Court. Such cases are conducted successfully, of course, but for the regular exporter or importer this is a highly daunting and potentially very expensive prospect, and, in the case of Japan, slow prospect.

10.47 How will one of those parties proceed? Probably the only way is to approach a lawyer in their own country to either seek a corresponding lawyer in Japan or recommend such a lawyer if they know of one.

10.48 Either way, it portends significant expense, uncertainty, and unpredictable time in reaching an uncertain result.

10.49 It is theoretically possible for a defendant to claim '*forum non conveniens*' (Latin for 'an inconvenient forum'[4]), but this normally requires that the defendant persuade the 'inconvenient' Court to rule that another forum is more appropriate.

10.50 Hence, the claimant has no real chance of making the situation 'convenient' for itself.

10.51 Some bill of lading or waybill conditions provide that the carrier is free to agree a different forum, but such requests appear to never find favour with carriers in our sector of commerce.

Solicitors and litigation

Choice of lawyers

10.52 At this point, the choice of lawyers becomes vital, since there are instances of a law firm taking on a case, and whilst otherwise well-versed in probate, general contract, and divorce matters, etc., fails to understand the issues involved, fails to recognise the applicable law, and provides a misdirected, expensive, and wasteful result.

10.53 Litigation has been commenced in County Courts on more than one occasion beyond the time-bars mentioned above and proceeded some distance before the carrier's legal representatives bring the attention of the judge to the fact there is no case to be answered.

10.54 Accordingly, it may not be advisable to approach your solicitor who may have served you well in corporate matters, and there is no real substitute for law firms large enough to have their own marine and air cargo department, and these firms are who you should be seeking.

4 Modern usage of the word 'forum' is multiple. In our context, it can mean simply a 'place' or 'location'.

Broad outline of events during litigation with costs implications

10.55 When considering that there appears to be no alternative to 'going legal', the threat of unpredictable costs rears its head.

10.56 Fear of costs with your own lawyer is one thing, but then, depending on the jurisdiction, there is the possibility of the defendant's costs if you lose.

10.57 Clearly, there is truth in this, but we can demystify how costs arise – the following exposition is based on English[5] practice, but undoubtedly has similarities with many other States.

10.58 This exposition follows events through to trial and final judgment – but it is also the case that they can be interrupted at any time, should either side decide to bring a conclusion – either to withdraw, settle, or seek a compromise with its opponent.

Pre-legal action

10.59 Having regard to comments above concerning the choice of lawyers, it is not unreasonable to ask if he or she is prepared to review your case and give an indication of his or her confidence (or lack thereof) in ultimate success.

10.60 At the same time, hourly rates should be advised, and (if relevant) those of an assistant whom may be brought into the case.

10.61 It is possible that some lawyers will be prepared to act on a 'contingency fee basis', also known more familiarly as 'no win/no fee'. In England, many lawyers appear to be reluctant to do this in the shipping/air cargo context, but it is worth asking about the possibility.

10.62 Should your lawyer be able to agree to this, you are almost certainly going to have to pay whatever disbursements may arise, such as Court fees and experts' fees – if there is a need to engage such professional advice.

10.63 Having formally instructed your lawyer to act for you, you will be 'on the clock', as it is often known. Your lawyer now commences to charge you by the hour for the time he or she spends on your case.

10.64 It is probable that he or she will wish to submit, and hence, he or she submits an interim invoice, on a regular basis, which should be accompanied by the record of time input, which during this period will comprise close study of your case, calling for additional documents if such are needed, etc.

10.65 He or she will approach the carrier with clearly stated arguments, in the attempt to get them to agree settlement.

Legal action

10.66 If your lawyer's efforts do not bear fruit, he or she will check with you, and advise that it is necessary to issue Court proceedings and ask for your concurrence.

10.67 The general outline of events which follows is based on procedure in the English Court. Courts in other States will have their own procedures and rules, but in the most general sense those Courts will conduct cases in comparable ways.

5 The English Court is separate, for instance, from the Scottish, which is why you may see on the reverse of the bill of lading conditions that the carrier sets down the English Court for any cases against it to be heard.

10.68 Your solicitor will 'draft the pleadings', as it is termed in England, which means that he or she will complete a 'Court claim form' showing you, the claimant (plaintiff), and the carrier (defendant or respondent), as the parties in dispute.

10.69 A document is drawn up to accompany the Court claim form, which is called the 'Particulars of Claim' in which will be set out all the relevant details of the claim which includes citing the relevant laws involved, the grounds for the claim, and the amount of the claim, properly explained.

10.70 The documents are then taken to the Court and officially 'issued', a Court fee having been paid.

10.71 Service of these documents on the carrier is then arranged – in smaller cases, service is effected by the Court office.

10.72 From this point onwards, the claimant is at risk of having to pay the defendant's costs, if it either loses or decides to withdraw from the action – such costs should be broadly similar to the claimant's own, and the claimant's lawyer should be able to give a general idea of how much may be involved at any given point.

10.73 There is a given amount of time allowed for the defendant to acknowledge service and submit a defence.

10.74 In the absence of acknowledgement and defence, it is open to the claimant to apply for 'Summary Judgment' – but it is always possible for the defendant to apply to have that judgment set aside, but it must provide a detailed explanation to the Court, and cover the costs of doing so.

10.75 Once the Court claim form and particulars are served, the Court commences to apply a timetable for the action to proceed. Forms are sent out and both sides must complete and return them to the Court – details required relate to whether expert witnesses are required, who may or may not appear as regular witnesses, and when they may or may not be available, and so on.

10.76 A judge will then examine the case on the basis of what is to hand, and set down Court directions, which will relate to exchange of documents by the parties to the dispute, and a trial date.

Part 36 offers

10.77 In English Civil Procedural Rules, there is a concept known as a 'Part 36 offer'.

10.78 This can be made at any time by either party, wherein it offers to settle at a lesser figure than claimed, on the understanding that if the other side accepts the offer, the offeree's costs will be reimbursed in addition to the settlement.

10.79 This is often a way to avoid trial and save mounting costs for both sides.

10.80 However, if the party who receives the offer, rejects it, and elects to go for trial, and does not succeed in obtaining judgment for more than the amount which has been offered, then the party who refused the offer will have to pay the offeror's costs.

Preparation for trial

10.81 At this point, costs can mount significantly, because your lawyer will be engaged in careful preparation of documents in the most diligent presentation for the judge to study and refer to during the trial and afterwards whilst considering his judgment.

10.82 In the lower Courts, the solicitor may have the 'right of audience' which means that he can argue his client's case directly.

10.83 If the case is for a large amount or complex, your solicitor will engage 'counsel' (a barrister specialising in this particular branch of the law) and instruct him on the case, and the counsel's fees will now be added to your costs.

10.84 Counsel will study the case and will advise his or her own views as to likely success.

Trial

10.85 It is well-illustrated in popular entertainment that attending a trial and watching the proceedings when one has a stake in the outcome is daunting, but strong nerves are definitely required, and there really is no alternative.

10.86 For the time being, continuing with that 'large' case, counsel for both sides will set out their arguments and will call witnesses and cross-examine.

10.87 The judge directs proceedings, and both counsels must defer to him and keep within strict guidelines. Straying outside of them will incur censure from the judge.

10.88 When all arguments are concluded, the trial ends, and the judge will retire to consider his verdict, which may be rendered some time – weeks or months – after the trial.

Costs awards

10.89 We have reached the point at which a verdict is handed down.

10.90 The winners are almost certainly going to ask for their costs. In the English Courts, they cannot expect to receive all of their costs, and in general terms a half to two-thirds is the rule.

Withdrawing at any stage

10.91 Clearly, all these factors must be considered most carefully when a claimant contemplates legal action.

10.92 However, as above, claimants must not overlook the fact that they can interrupt the process at any stage, but the party withdrawing is likely to face a demand from the other side for its costs to date to be paid – that will be the price for 'getting out' of a situation which may have increasingly discouraging prospects of failure or appear to be hopeless.

Annexes

Each of the following is an example only, which should be adapted to your particular requirements, of course. They are intended as helpful guides only.

Examples of claim notices

Air claim notice

Your Company Name

From:	*Your Name*	*Address*	
Any queries?	Call: #### ##### Mobile: #### ##### e-Mail: ###@###		
To:		Title:	
Company:			
Date:		Our ref:	

NOTICE OF CLAIM

Dear

Air waybill no.	
Cargo	# pcs/# kg
Commodity	
Airport of delivery	
Date of delivery	

The above consignment has been received in a damaged condition, and in due course, we will be submitting a claim for compensation.

We also give notice on behalf of the shipper, insofar as they have any rights of claim.

PERCEIVED CAUSE OF LOSS:

########

SURVEY:

You are invited to inspect the consignment which is currently at the premises of ######, located at ######.

It will remain there for so long as is practical, having regard to its present condition, and the need to effect salvage sales, if possible.

ABC Surveys Ltd will carry out a survey on our behalf. They will be happy to liaise with you and/or your representative hopefully for a joint inspection.

Their phone details are: office ######, cell/mobile #######.

If you choose not to carry out a survey, we will assume that the conclusions of our surveyor will be accepted as binding.

Kind regards,
Signature

Ocean claim notice

Your Company Name

From:	*Your Name*	*Address*
Any queries?	Call: #### ##### Mobile: #### ##### e-Mail: xxxxx@xxxx.com	

To:		Title:	
Company:			
Date:		Our ref:	

NOTICE OF CLAIM

Dear

Vessel and voyage no.	
Port and date of discharge	
Bill of lading no.	
Container no.	
Commodity	
Received at	
Date and time of receipt	

The above consignment has been received in a damaged condition, and in due course, we will be submitting a claim for compensation.

We also give notice on behalf of the shipper, insofar as they have any rights of claim.

PERCEIVED CAUSE OF LOSS:

######

SURVEY:

You are invited to inspect the consignment which is currently at the premises of ######, located at ######.

It will remain there for so long as is practical, having regard to its present condition, and the need to effect salvage sales, if possible.

ABC Surveys Ltd will carry out a survey on behalf of my client, and they will be happy to liaise with you and/or your representative hopefully for a joint inspection. Their phone details are: office #### ######, cell/mobile #### ######.

If you choose not to carry out a survey, we will assume that the conclusions of our surveyor will be accepted as binding.

Kind regards,
Signature

Non-survey claim notice

If you have decided that you do not require a surveyor to act for you, you should substitute the following wording in the body of the notice of claim.

> The above consignment has been received in a damaged condition, and in due course, we will be submitting a claim for compensation.
> We also give notice on behalf of the shipper, insofar as they have any rights of claim.
> PERCEIVED CAUSE OF LOSS:
> #######
> SURVEY:
> You are invited to inspect the consignment which is currently at the premises of ######, located at ######.
> Your contact will be Mr/Ms ######; phone contacts are office: ######, cell/mobile: ######.

Claim submission covering letter or message

Air claim

Your ref:
Our ref:

XYZ Airline
Cargo Claims Department
Sent by email to: ######.#####@#####.com

Saturday, 17 April 2021
Dear sirs,
AWB: ###/#### ####
CARTONS: *COMMODITY*
DELIVERED AT: *AIRPORT*
CAUSE OF DAMAGE: ######
CLAIM VALUE: UK£ #########

We herewith submit our claim for compensation on the above consignment.
On arrival at our/our receivers' premises, the consignment was found to be ###########.
The damage was confirmed by professional survey, and it was not possible to achieve any salvage, and consequently, the consignment was disposed of without sales.
OR
The damage was confirmed by professional survey, and a salvage operation was initiated resulting in ##% of the consignment able to be sold and the remainder having to be dumped.
Accordingly, the losses sustained are as shown on the attached quantum calculation.
Various documents are also attached to support our client's submission, and we request your settlement proposals as soon as possible, please.

Yours faithfully,
COMPANY NAME
SIGNED

Attachments:

1. Calculation of quantum
    a. Evidence of arrived-sound market value – copy sales invoices, proving sound market prices, or official price list
    b. Evidence of arrived-damaged market value – copy sales invoices for all salvage sales OR proof of nil salvage value
    c. Survey fee invoice
    d. Expenses arising directly from the loss – sorting/repacking/dumping costs – supported by invoices
2. Survey report with all other documents

Ocean claim

Your ref:
Our ref:

CDE Ocean Carrier
Cargo Claims Department
Sent by email to: ######.#####@#####.com
Saturday, 17 April 2021

Dear sirs,
VESSEL: *NAME* – DISCHARGED AT: *PORT/DATE*
BILL OF LADING OR WAYBILL NO.: #### - CONTAINER NO.: ####
CARTONS OF
RECEIVED WITH TEMPERATURE ABUSE
CLAIM VALUE: UK£ #####

We herewith submit our claim for compensation on the above consignment.
On arrival at our/our receivers' premises, the consignment was found to be ###########.
The shipper has provided evidence of both export quality and correct temperature at the time of delivery to the load port.
The damage was confirmed by professional survey, and it was not possible to achieve any salvage, and consequently, the consignment was disposed of without sales.
OR
The damage was confirmed by professional survey, and a salvage operation was initiated resulting in ##% of the consignment able to be sold and the remainder having to be dumped.
Accordingly, the losses sustained are as shown on the attached quantum calculation. Various documents are also attached to support our client's submission, and I request your settlement proposals as soon as possible, please.

Yours faithfully,
COMPANY NAME
SIGNED

Attachments:

2. Calculation of quantum
   a. Evidence of arrived-sound market value – copy sales invoices, proving sound market prices, or official price list
   b. Evidence of arrived-damaged market value – copy sales invoices for all salvage sales OR proof of nil salvage value
   c. Survey fee invoice
   d. Expenses arising directly from the loss – sorting/repacking/dumping costs – supported by invoices
3. Survey report with all other documents

Excel spreadsheet to show quantum

Quantum					
Number of cartons	Commodity	Per carton price	Value	Total value	Refer to attachment
Arrived-sound market value					
			€0.00		2a
			€0.00		
0	Total number of cartons				
Total value				€0.00	
Less: arrived-damaged market value					
Total salvage sales					2b
Nett loss of value				€0.00	
Plus: wasted expenses/expenses unavoidably arising					
Survey fees			€0.00		2c
Sorting and repacking			€0.00		2d
Dumping costs			€0.00		2e
Total expenses				€0.00	
Total claimed amount				€0.00	

Cession of rights wording

There are many different versions of these wordings, and here are two examples which will suffice for these purposes.

Air

> Waiver and authorisation
>
> TO: *Consignee or shipper's name* AWB NO: AWB number
>
> We hereby waive all rights and remedies arising under the above air waybill in favour of *consignee or shipper's name.*
>
> We also record that *consignee or shipper's name* has the authority to use our name to the extent necessary effectively to exercise all or any of such rights and remedies; that we will furnish you with any assistance you may reasonably require of us when exercising such rights and remedies on the understanding that you will indemnify us against any liability for costs, charges, and expenses arising in connection with any proceedings which you may take in our name in the exercise of such rights and remedies.
>
> Signed: ______________________ Date: ______________
>
> Company: ______________________ Name ______________
>
> Position: ______________
>
> *COMPANY STAMP/SEAL – if applicable*

Ocean

> Waiver and authorisation
>
> VESSEL NAME: ####/VOYAGE NUMBER/####
> DISCHARGED AT PORT: #### – DATE ##4TH #####, ####
> BILL OF LADING OR SEA WAYBILL NO. #####/CONTAINER NO. #####
> #### CARTONS OF #####
>
> We, *shipper's or consignee's name*, hereby waive all rights and remedies arising under the above bill of lading/sea waybill in favour of *exporter's/importer's name.*
>
> We also record that *exporter's/importer's name* has the authority to use our name to the extent necessary effectively to exercise all or any of such rights and remedies; that we will furnish any assistance which may reasonably be required of us when exercising such rights and remedies.
>
> Signed: ______________________ Date: ______________
>
> Company: ______________________ Name ______________
>
> Position: ______________
>
> *COMPANY STAMP/SEAL – if applicable*

Schedules

Air

Montreal Convention

Montreal Convention 1999

CHAPTER I

General Provisions

Article 1 — Scope of Application

1. This Convention applies to all international carriage of persons, baggage or cargo performed by aircraft for reward. It applies equally to gratuitous carriage by aircraft performed by an air transport undertaking.
2. For the purposes of this Convention, the expression *international carriage* means any carriage in which, according to the agreement between the parties, the place of departure and the place of destination, whether or not there be a break in the carriage or a transhipment, are situated either within the territories of two States Parties, or within the territory of a single State Party if there is an agreed stopping place within the territory of another State, even if that State is not a State Party. Carriage between two points within the territory of a single State Party without an agreed stopping place within the territory of another State is not international carriage for the purposes of this Convention.
3. Carriage to be performed by several successive carriers is deemed, for the purposes of this Convention, to be one undivided carriage if it has been regarded by the parties as a single operation, whether it had been agreed upon under the form of a single contract or of a series of contracts, and it does not lose its international character merely because one contract or a series of contracts is to be performed entirely within the territory of the same State.
4. This Convention applies also to carriage as set out in Chapter V, subject to the terms contained therein.

Article 2 — Carriage Performed by State and Carriage of Postal Items

1. This Convention applies to carriage performed by the State or by legally constituted public bodies provided it falls within the conditions laid down in Article 1.

2. In the carriage of postal items, the carrier shall be liable only to the relevant postal administration in accordance with the rules applicable to the relationship between the carriers and the postal administrations.
3. Except as provided in paragraph 2 of this Article, the provisions of this Convention shall not apply to the carriage of postal items.

CHAPTER II

Documentation and Duties of the Parties Relating to the Carriage of Passengers, Baggage and Cargo

Article 3 — Passengers and Baggage DELETED FOR PURPOSES OF THIS BOOK

Article 4 — Cargo

1. In respect of the carriage of cargo, an air waybill shall be delivered.
2. Any other means which preserves a record of the carriage to be performed may be substituted for the delivery of an air waybill. If such other means are used, the carrier shall, if so requested by the consignor, deliver to the consignor a cargo receipt permitting identification of the consignment and access to the information contained in the record preserved by such other means.

Article 5 — Contents of Air Waybill or Cargo Receipt The air waybill or the cargo receipt shall include:

a) an indication of the places of departure and destination;
b) if the places of departure and destination are within the territory of a single State Party, one or more agreed stopping places being within the territory of another State, an indication of at least one such stopping place; and
c) an indication of the weight of the consignment.

Article 6 - Document Relating to the Nature of the Cargo The consignor may be required, if necessary to meet the formalities of customs, police and similar public authorities, to deliver a document indicating the nature of the cargo. This provision creates for the carrier no duty, obligation or liability resulting therefrom.

Article 7 — Description of Air Waybill

1. The air waybill shall be made out by the consignor in three original parts.
2. The first part shall be marked 'for the carrier'; it shall be signed by the consignor. The second part shall be marked 'for the consignee'; it shall be signed by the consignor and by the carrier. The third part shall be signed by the carrier who shall hand it to the consignor after the cargo has been accepted.
3. The signature of the carrier and that of the consignor may be printed or stamped.
4. If, at the request of the consignor, the carrier makes out the air waybill, the carrier shall be deemed, subject to proof to the contrary, to have done so on behalf of the consignor.

Article 8 — Documentation for Multiple Packages When there is more than one package:

a) the carrier of cargo has the right to require the consignor to make out separate air waybills;

b) the consignor has the right to require the carrier to deliver separate cargo receipts when the other means referred to in paragraph 2 of Article 4 are used.

Article 9 — Non-compliance with Documentary Requirements Non-compliance with the provisions of Articles 4 to 8 shall not affect the existence or the validity of the contract of carriage, which shall, nonetheless, be subject to the rules of this Convention including those relating to limitation of liability.

Article 10 — Responsibility for Particulars of Documentation

1. The consignor is responsible for the correctness of the particulars and statements relating to the cargo inserted by it or on its behalf in the air waybill or furnished by it or on its behalf to the carrier for insertion in the cargo receipt or for insertion in the record preserved by the other means referred to in paragraph 2 of Article 4. The foregoing shall also apply where the person acting on behalf of the consignor is also the agent of the carrier.
2. The consignor shall indemnify the carrier against all damage suffered by it, or by any other person to whom the carrier is liable, by reason of the irregularity, incorrectness or incompleteness of the particulars and statements furnished by the consignor or on its behalf.
3. Subject to the provisions of paragraphs 1 and 2 of this Article, the carrier shall indemnify the consignor against all damage suffered by it, or by any other person to whom the consignor is liable, by reason of the irregularity, incorrectness or incompleteness of the particulars and statements inserted by the carrier or on its behalf in the cargo receipt or in the record preserved by the other means referred to in paragraph 2 of Article 4.

Article 11 — Evidentiary Value of Documentation

1. The air waybill or the cargo receipt is prima *facie* evidence of the conclusion of the contract, of the acceptance of the cargo and of the conditions of carriage mentioned therein.
2. Any statements in the air waybill or the cargo receipt relating to the weight, dimensions and packing of the cargo, as well as those relating to the number of packages, are *prima facie* evidence of the facts stated; those relating to the quantity, volume and condition of the cargo do not constitute evidence against the carrier except so far as they both have been and are stated in the air waybill or the cargo receipt to have been, checked by it in the presence of the consignor, or relate to the apparent condition of the cargo.

Article 12 — Right of Disposition of Cargo

1. Subject to its liability to carry out all its obligations under the contract of carriage, the consignor has the right to dispose of the cargo by withdrawing it at the airport of departure or destination, or by stopping it in the course of the journey on any landing, or by calling for it to be delivered at the place of destination or in the course of the journey to a person other than the consignee originally designated, or by requiring it to be returned to the airport of departure. The consignor must not exercise this right of disposition in such a way as to prejudice the carrier

or other consignors and must reimburse any expenses occasioned by the exercise of this right.

2. If it is impossible to carry out the instructions of the consignor, the carrier must so inform the consignor forthwith.
3. If the carrier carries out the instructions of the consignor for the disposition of the cargo without requiring the production of the part of the air waybill or the cargo receipt delivered to the latter, the carrier will be liable, without prejudice to its right of recovery from the consignor, for any damage which may be caused thereby to any person who is lawfully in possession of that part of the air waybill or the cargo receipt.
4. The right conferred on the consignor ceases at the moment when that of the consignee begins in accordance with Article 13. Nevertheless, if the consignee declines to accept the cargo, or cannot be communicated with, the consignor resumes its right of disposition.

Article 13 — Delivery of the Cargo

1. Except when the consignor has exercised its right under Article 12, the consignee is entitled, on arrival of the cargo at the place of destination, to require the carrier to deliver the cargo to it, on payment of the charges due and on complying with the conditions of carriage.
2. Unless it is otherwise agreed, it is the duty of the carrier to give notice to the consignee as soon as the cargo arrives.
3. If the carrier admits the loss of the cargo, or if the cargo has not arrived at the expiration of seven days after the date on which it ought to have arrived, the consignee is entitled to enforce against the carrier the rights which ß ow from the contract of carriage.

Article 14 — Enforcement of the Rights of Consignor and Consignee The consignor and the consignee can respectively enforce all the rights given to them by Articles 12 and 13, each in its own name, whether it is acting in its own interest or in the interest of another, provided that it carries out the obligations imposed by the contract of carriage.

Article 15 — Relations of Consignor and Consignee or Mutual Relations of Third Parties

1. Articles 12, 13 and 14 do not affect either the relations of the consignor and the consignee with each other or the mutual relations of third parties whose rights are derived either from the consignor or from the consignee.
2. The provisions of Articles 12, 13 and 14 can only be varied by express provision in the air waybill or the cargo receipt.

Article 16 — Formalities of Customs, Police or Other Public Authorities

1. The consignor must furnish such information and such documents as are necessary to meet the formalities of customs, police and any other public authorities before the cargo can be delivered to the consignee. The consignor is liable to the carrier for any damage occasioned by the absence, insufficiency or irregularity of

any such information or documents, unless the damage is due to the fault of the carrier, its servants or agents.

2. The carrier is under no obligation to enquire into the correctness or sufficiency of such information or documents.

CHAPTER III — Liability of the Carrier and Extent of Compensation for Damage

Article 17 — Death and Injury of Passengers — Damage to Baggage DELETED FOR THE PURPOSES OF THIS BOOK

Article 18 — Damage to Cargo

1. The carrier is liable for damage sustained in the event of the destruction or loss of, or damage to, cargo upon condition only that the event which caused the damage so sustained took place during the carriage by air.
2. However, the carrier is not liable if and to the extent it proves that the destruction, or loss of, or damage to, the cargo resulted from one or more of the following:
   a) inherent defect, quality or vice of that cargo;
   b) defective packing of that cargo performed by a person other than the carrier or its servants or agents;
   c) an act of war or an armed conflict;
   d) an act of public authority carried out in connection with the entry, exit or transit of the cargo.
3. The carriage by air within the meaning of paragraph 1 of this Article comprises the period during which the cargo is in the charge of the carrier.
4. The period of the carriage by air does not extend to any carriage by land, by sea or by inland waterway performed outside an airport. If, however, such carriage takes place in the performance of a contract for carriage by air, for the purpose of loading, delivery or transhipment, any damage is presumed, subject to proof to the contrary, to have been the result of an event which took place during the carriage by air. If a carrier, without the consent of the consignor, substitutes carriage by another mode of transport for the whole or part of a carriage intended by the agreement between the parties to be carriage by air, such carriage by another mode of transport is deemed to be within the period of carriage by air.

Article 19 — Delay The carrier is liable for damage occasioned by delay in the carriage by air of passengers, baggage or cargo. Nevertheless, the carrier shall not be liable for damage occasioned by delay if it proves that it and its servants and agents took all measures that could reasonably be required to avoid the damage or that it was impossible for it or them to take such measures.

Article 20 — Exoneration If the carrier proves that the damage was caused or contributed to by the negligence or other wrongful act or omission of the person claiming compensation, or the person from whom he or she derives his or her rights, the carrier shall be wholly or partly exonerated from its liability to the claimant to the extent that such negligence or wrongful act or omission caused or contributed to the damage. When by reason of death or injury of a passenger compensation is claimed by a person other than the passenger, the carrier shall likewise be wholly or partly exonerated from its liability to the extent that it proves that the damage was caused or contributed to by the negligence or other wrongful act or omission of that passenger. This Article applies to all the liability provisions in this Convention, including paragraph 1 of Article 21.

Article 21 — Compensation in Case of Death or Injury of Passengers DELETED FOR THE PURPOSES OF THIS BOOK

Article 22 — Limits of Liability in Relation to Delay, Baggage and Cargo

1. DELETED FOR THE PURPOSES OF THIS BOOK [Delay to Passengers].
2. DELETED FOR THE PURPOSES OF THIS BOOK [Baggage]
3. In the carriage of cargo, the liability of the carrier in the case of destruction, loss, damage or delay is limited to a sum of 17 Special Drawing Rights per kilogramme, unless the consignor has made, at the time when the package was handed over to the carrier, a special declaration of interest in delivery at destination and has paid a supplementary sum if the case so requires. In that case the carrier will be liable to pay a sum not exceeding the declared sum, unless it proves that the sum is greater than the consignor's actual interest in delivery at destination.
4. In the case of destruction, loss, damage or delay of part of the cargo, or of any object contained therein, the weight to be taken into consideration in determining the amount to which the carrier's liability is limited shall be only the total weight of the package or packages concerned. Nevertheless, when the destruction, loss, damage or delay of a part of the cargo, or of an object contained therein, affects the value of other packages covered by the same air waybill, or the same receipt or, if they were not issued, by the same record preserved by the other means referred to in paragraph 2 of Article 4, the total weight of such package or packages shall also be taken into consideration in determining the limit of liability.
5. The foregoing provisions of paragraphs 1 and 2 of this Article shall not apply if it is proved that the damage resulted from an act or omission of the carrier, its servants or agents, done with intent to cause damage or recklessly and with knowledge that damage would probably result; provided that, in the case of such act or omission of a servant or agent, it is also proved that such servant or agent was acting within the scope of its employment.
6. The limits prescribed in Article 21 and in this Article shall not prevent the court from awarding, in accordance with its own law, in addition, the whole or part of the court costs and of the other expenses of the litigation incurred by the plaintiff, including interest. The foregoing provision shall not apply if the amount of the damages awarded, excluding court costs and other expenses of the litigation, does not exceed the sum which the carrier has offered in writing to the plaintiff within a period of six months from the date of the occurrence causing the damage, or before the commencement of the action, if that is later.

Article 23 — Conversion of Monetary Units DELETED FOR PURPOSES OF THIS BOOK

Article 24 — Review of Limits DELETED FOR PURPOSES OF THIS BOOK

Article 25 — Stipulation on Limits A carrier may stipulate that the contract of carriage shall be subject to higher limits of liability than those provided for in this Convention or to no limits of liability whatsoever.

Article 26 — Invalidity of Contractual Provisions Any provision tending to relieve the carrier of liability or to fix a lower limit than that which is laid down in this Convention shall be null and void, but the nullity of any such provision does not involve the nullity of the whole contract, which shall remain subject to the provisions of this Convention.

Article 27 — Freedom to Contract Nothing contained in this Convention shall prevent the carrier from refusing to enter into any contract of carriage, from waiving any defences available under the Convention, or from laying down conditions which do not conflict with the provisions of this Convention.

Article 28 — Advance Payments DELETED FOR PURPOSES OF THIS BOOK

Article 29 — Basis of Claims In the carriage of passengers, baggage and cargo, any action for damages, however founded, whether under this Convention or in contract or in tort or otherwise, can only be brought subject to the conditions and such limits of liability as are set out in this Convention without prejudice to the question as to who are the persons who have the right to bring suit and what are their respective rights. In any such action, punitive, exemplary or any other non-compensatory damages shall not be recoverable.

Article 30 Servants, Agents — Aggregation of Claims
DELETED FOR PURPOSES OF THIS BOOK

Article 31 — Timely Notice of Complaints

1. Receipt by the person entitled to delivery of checked baggage or cargo without complaint is *prima facie* evidence that the same has been delivered in good condition and in accordance with the document of carriage or with the record preserved by the other means referred to in paragraph 2 of Article 3 and paragraph 2 of Article 4.
2. In the case of damage, the person entitled to delivery must complain to the carrier forthwith after the discovery of the damage, and, at the latest, within seven days from the date of receipt in the case of checked baggage and fourteen days from the date of receipt in the case of cargo. In the case of delay, the complaint must be made at the latest within twenty-one days from the date on which the baggage or cargo have been placed at his or her disposal.
3. Every complaint must be made in writing and given or dispatched within the times aforesaid.
4. If no complaint is made within the times aforesaid, no action shall lie against the carrier, save in the case of fraud on its part.

Article 32 — Death of Person Liable In the case of the death of the person liable, an action for damages lies in accordance with the terms of this Convention against those legally representing his or her estate.[1]

1 This can be taken to mean that if a carrier ceases trading, or is forced into liquidation, the claim continues against the carrier.

Article 33 — Jurisdiction

1. An action for damages must be brought, at the option of the plaintiff, in the territory of one of the States Parties, either before the court of the domicile of the carrier or of its principal place of business, or where it has a place of business through which the contract has been made or before the court at the place of destination.
2. DELETED FOR PURPOSES OF THIS BOOK [special arrangements for passenger claims]
3. DELETED FOR PURPOSES OF THIS BOOK [deals with the immediately preceding paragraph]

Article 34 — Arbitration

1. Subject to the provisions of this Article, the parties to the contract of carriage for cargo may stipulate that any dispute relating to the liability of the carrier under this Convention shall be settled by arbitration. Such agreement shall be in writing.
2. The arbitration proceedings shall, at the option of the claimant, take place within one of the jurisdictions referred to in Article 33.
3. The arbitrator or arbitration tribunal shall apply the provisions of this Convention.
4. The provisions of paragraphs 2 and 3 of this Article shall be deemed to be part of every arbitration clause or agreement, and any term of such clause or agreement which is inconsistent therewith shall be null and void.

Article 35 — Limitation of Actions

1. The right to damages shall be extinguished if an action is not brought within a period of two years, reckoned from the date of arrival at the destination, or from the date on which the aircraft ought to have arrived, or from the date on which the carriage stopped.
2. The method of calculating that period shall be determined by the law of the court seized of the case.

Article 36 — Successive Carriage

1. In the case of carriage to be performed by various successive carriers and falling within the definition set out in paragraph 3 of Article 1, each carrier which accepts passengers, baggage or cargo is subject to the rules set out in this Convention and is deemed to be one of the parties to the contract of carriage in so far as the contract deals with that part of the carriage which is performed under its supervision.
2. DELETED FOR PURPOSES OF THIS BOOK [passenger provisions]
3. As regards baggage or cargo, the passenger or consignor will have a right of action against the 1st carrier, and the passenger or consignee who is entitled to delivery will have a right of action against the last carrier, and further, each may take action against the carrier which performed the carriage during which the destruction, loss, damage or delay took place. These carriers will be jointly and severally liable to the passenger or to the consignor or consignee.

Article 37 — Right of Recourse against Third Parties

Nothing in this Convention shall prejudice the question whether a person liable for damage in accordance with its provisions has a right of recourse against any other person.

CHAPTER IV — Combined Carriage

Article 38 — Combined Carriage

1. In the case of combined carriage performed partly by air and partly by any other mode of carriage, the provisions of this Convention shall, subject to paragraph 4 of Article 18, apply only to the carriage by air, provided that the carriage by air falls within the terms of Article 1.
2. Nothing in this Convention shall prevent the parties in the case of combined carriage from inserting in the document of air carriage conditions relating to other modes of carriage, provided that the provisions of this Convention are observed as regards the carriage by air.

CHAPTER V

Carriage by Air Performed by Person other than the Contracting Carrier

Article 39 — Contracting Carrier — Actual Carrier The provisions of this Chapter apply when a person (hereinafter referred to as 'the contracting carrier') as a principal makes a contract of carriage governed by this Convention with a passenger or consignor or with a person acting on behalf of the passenger or consignor, and another person (hereinafter referred to as 'the actual carrier') performs, by virtue of authority from the contracting carrier, the whole or part of the carriage, but is not with respect to such part a successive carrier within the meaning of this Convention. Such authority shall be presumed in the absence of proof to the contrary.

Article 40 — Respective Liability of Contracting and Actual Carriers If an actual carrier performs the whole or part of carriage which, according to the contract referred to in Article 39, is governed by this Convention, both the contracting carrier and the actual carrier shall, except as otherwise provided in this Chapter, be subject to the rules of this Convention, the former for the whole of the carriage contemplated in the contract, the latter solely for the carriage which it performs.

Article 41 — Mutual Liability

1. The acts and omissions of the actual carrier and of its servants and agents acting within the scope of their employment shall, in relation to the carriage performed by the actual carrier, be deemed to be also those of the contracting carrier.
2. The acts and omissions of the contracting carrier and of its servants and agents acting within the scope of their employment shall, in relation to the carriage performed by the actual carrier, be deemed to be also those of the actual carrier. Nevertheless, no such act or omission shall subject the actual carrier to liability exceeding the amounts referred to in Articles 21, 22, 23 and 24. Any special agreement under which the contracting carrier assumes obligations not imposed by this Convention or any waiver of rights or defences conferred by this

Convention or any special declaration of interest in delivery at destination contemplated in Article 22 shall not affect the actual carrier unless agreed to by it.

Article 42 — Addressee of Complaints and Instructions Any complaint to be made or instruction to be given under this Convention to the carrier shall have the same effect whether addressed to the contracting carrier or to the actual carrier. Nevertheless, instructions referred to in Article 12 shall only be effective if addressed to the contracting carrier.

Article 43 — Servants and Agents In relation to the carriage performed by the actual carrier, any servant or agent of that carrier or of the contracting carrier shall, if they prove that they acted within the scope of their employment, be entitled to avail themselves of the conditions and limits of liability which are applicable under this Convention to the carrier whose servant or agent they are, unless it is proved that they acted in a manner that prevents the limits of liability from being invoked in accordance with this Convention.

Article 44 — Aggregation of Damages In relation to the carriage performed by the actual carrier, the aggregate of the amounts recoverable from that carrier and the contracting carrier, and from their servants and agents acting within the scope of their employment, shall not exceed the highest amount which could be awarded against either the contracting carrier or the actual carrier under this Convention, but none of the persons mentioned shall be liable for a sum in excess of the limit applicable to that person.

Article 45 — Addressee of Claims In relation to the carriage performed by the actual carrier, an action for damages may be brought, at the option of the plaintiff, against that carrier or the contracting carrier, or against both together or separately. If the action is brought against only one of those carriers, that carrier shall have the right to require the other carrier to be joined in the proceedings, the procedure and effects being governed by the law of the court seized of the case.

Article 46 — Additional Jurisdiction THE REMAINING ARTICLES ARE DELETED FOR THE PURPOSES OF THIS BOOK AS THEY WILL ALMOST NEVER BE RELEVANT TO CLAIMANTS

Warsaw/Hague

The Warsaw Convention as amended at The Hague 1955

Chapter I – Scope – Definitions

Article 1

1. This Convention applies to all international carriage of persons, baggage or cargo performed by aircraft for reward. It applies equally to gratuitous carriage by aircraft performed by an air transport undertaking.
2. For the purposes of this Convention, the expression international carriage means any carriage in which, according to the agreement between the parties, the place of departure and the place of destination, whether or not there be a break in the carriage or a transhipment, are situated either within the territories of two High Contracting Parties or within the territory of a single High Contracting Party if there is an agreed stopping place within the territory of another State, even if that State is not a High Contracting Party. Carriage between two points within the territory of a single High Contracting Party without an agreed stopping place within the territory of another State is not international carriage for the purposes of this Convention.
3. Carriage to be performed by several successive air carriers is deemed, for the purposes of this Convention, to be one undivided carriage if it has been regarded by the parties as a single operation, whether it had been agreed upon under the form of a single contract or of a series of contracts, and it does not lose its international character merely because one contract or a series of contracts is to be performed entirely within the territory of the same State.

Article 2

1. The Convention applies to carriage performed by the State or by legally constituted public bodies provided it falls within the conditions laid down in Article 1.
2. This Convention shall not apply to carriage of mail and postal packages.

Chapter II – Documents of Carriage

SECTION 1 – PASSENGER TICKET

Article 3 DELETED FOR PURPOSES OF THIS BOOK

SECTION 2 – BAGGAGE CHECK

Article 4 DELETED FOR PURPOSES OF THIS BOOK

SECTION 3 – AIR WAYBILL

Article 5

1. Every carrier of cargo has the right to require the consignor to make out and hand over to him a document called an 'air waybill'; every consignor has the right to require the carrier to accept this document.

2. The absence, irregularity or loss of this document does not affect the existence or the validity of the contract of carriage which shall, subject to the provisions of Article 9, be none the less governed by the rules of this Convention.

Article 6

1. The air waybill shall be made out by the consignor in three original parts and be handed over with the cargo.
2. The first part shall be marked 'for the carrier' and shall be signed by the consignor. The second part shall be marked 'for the consignee'; it shall be signed by the consignor and by the carrier and shall accompany the cargo. The third part shall be signed by the carrier and handed by him to the consignor after the cargo has been accepted.
3. The carrier shall sign prior to the loading of the cargo on board the aircraft.
4. The signature of the carrier may be stamped; that of the consignor may be printed or stamped.
5. If, at the request of the consignor, the carrier makes out the air waybill, he shall be deemed, subject to proof to the contrary, to have done so on behalf of the consignor.

Article 7 The carrier of cargo has the right to require the consignor to make out separate air waybills when there is more than one package.

Article 8 The air waybill shall contain:

(a) an indication of the places of departure and destination;
(b) if the places of departure and destination are within the territory of a single High Contracting Party[2], one or more agreed stopping places being within the territory of another State, an indication of at least one such stopping place;
(c) a notice to the consignor to the effect that, if the carriage involves an ultimate destination or stop in a country other than the country of departure, the Warsaw Convention may be applicable, and that the Convention governs and, in most cases, limits the liability of carriers in respect of loss of or damage to cargo.

Article 9 If, with the consent of the carrier, cargo is loaded on board the aircraft without an air waybill having been made out, or if the air waybill does not include the notice required by Article 8, paragraph (c), the carrier shall not be entitled to avail himself of the provisions of Article 22, paragraph 2.

Article 10

1. The consignor is responsible for the correctness of the particulars and statements relating to the cargo which he inserts in the air waybill.
2. The consignor shall indemnify the carrier against all damage suffered by him, or by any other person to whom the carrier is liable, by reason of the irregularity, incorrectness or incompleteness of the particulars and statements furnished by the consignor.

2 A High Contracting Party can be regarded as a State. See Article 40A below.

Article 11

1. The air waybill is prima facie evidence of the conclusion of the contract, of the receipt of the cargo and of the conditions of carriage.
2. The statements in the air waybill relating to the weight, dimensions and packing of the cargo, as well as those relating to the number of packages, are prima facie evidence of the facts stated; those relating to the quantity, volume and condition of the cargo do not constitute evidence against the carrier except so far as they both have been and are stated in the air waybill to have been, checked by him in the presence of the consignor, or relate to the apparent condition of the cargo.

Article 12

1. Subject to his liability to carry out all his obligations under the contract of carriage, the consignor has the right to dispose of the cargo by withdrawing it at the aerodrome of departure or destination, or by stopping it in the course of the journey on any landing, or by calling for it to be delivered at the place of destination or in the course of the journey to a person other than the consignee named in the air waybill, or by requiring it to be returned to the aerodrome of departure. He must not exercise this right of disposition in such a way as to prejudice the carrier or other consignors and he must repay any expenses occasioned by the exercise of this right.
2. If it is impossible to carry out the orders of the consignor the carrier must so inform him forthwith.
3. If the carrier obeys the orders of the consignor for the disposition of the cargo without requiring the production of the part of the air waybill delivered to the latter, he will be liable, without prejudice to his right of recovery from the consignor, for any damage which may be caused thereby to any person who is lawfully in possession of that part of the air waybill.
4. The right conferred on the consignor ceases at the moment when that of the consignee begins in accordance with Article 13. Nevertheless, if the consignee declines to accept the air waybill or the cargo, or if he cannot be communicated with, the consignor resumes his right of disposition.

Article 13

1. Except in the circumstances set out in the preceding Article, the consignee is entitled, on arrival of the cargo at the place of destination, to require the carrier to hand over to him the air waybill and to deliver the cargo to him, on payment of the charges due and on complying with the conditions of carriage set out in the air waybill.
2. Unless it is otherwise agreed, it is the duty of the carrier to give notice to the consignee as soon as the cargo arrives.
3. If the carrier admits the loss of the cargo, or if the cargo has not arrived at the expiration of seven days after the date on which it ought to have arrived, the consignee is entitled to put into force against the carrier the rights which flow from the contract of carriage.

Article 14 The consignor and the consignee can respectively enforce all the rights given them by Articles 12 and 13, each in his own name, whether he is acting in his own interest or in the interest of another, provided that he carries out the obligations imposed by the contract.

Article 15

1. Articles 12, 13 and 14 do not affect either the relations of the consignor or the consignee with each other or the mutual relations of third parties whose rights are derived either from the consignor or from the consignee.
2. The provisions of Articles 12, 13 and 14 can only be varied by express provision in the air waybill.
3. Nothing in this Convention prevents the issue of a negotiable air waybill.

Article 16

1. The consignor must furnish such information and attach to the air waybill such documents as are necessary to meet the formalities of customs, octroi or police before the cargo can be delivered to the consignee. The consignor is liable to the carrier for any damage occasioned by the absence, insufficiency or irregularity of any such information or documents, unless the damage is due to the fault of the carrier or his servants or agents.
2. The carrier is under no obligation to inquire into the correctness or sufficiency of such information or documents.

Chapter III – Liability of the Carrier

Article 17 DELETED FOR PURPOSES OF THIS BOOK

Article 18

1. The carrier is liable for damages sustained in the event of the destruction or loss of, or of damage to, any registered baggage or any cargo, if the occurrence which caused the damage so sustained took place during the carriage by air.
2. The carriage by air within the meaning of the preceding paragraph comprises the period during which the baggage or cargo is in charge of the carrier, whether in an aerodrome or on board an aircraft, or, in the case of a landing outside an aerodrome, in any place whatsoever.
3. The period of the carriage by air does not extend to any carriage by land, by sea or by river performed outside an aerodrome. If, however, such a carriage takes place in the performance of a contract for carriage by air, for the purpose of loading, delivery or trans-shipment, any damage is presumed, subject to proof to the contrary, to have been the result of an event which took place during the carriage by air.

Article 19 The carrier is liable for damage occasioned by delay in the carriage by air of passengers, baggage or cargo.

Article 20 The carrier is not liable if he proves that he and his servants and agents have taken all necessary measures to avoid the damage or that it was impossible for him or them to take such measures.

Article 21 If the carrier proves that the damage was caused by or contributed to by the negligence of the injured person the Court may, in accordance with the provisions of its own law, exonerate the carrier wholly or partly from his liability.

Article 22

1. In the carriage of persons the liability of the carrier for each passenger is limited to the sum of two hundred and fifty thousand francs. Where, in accordance with the law of the court seized of the case, damages may be awarded in the form of periodical payments, the equivalent capital value of the said payments shall not exceed two hundred and fifty thousand francs. Nevertheless, by special contract, the carrier and the passenger may agree to a higher limit of liability.
2. (a) In the carriage of registered baggage and of cargo, the liability of the carrier is limited to a sum of two hundred and fifty francs per kilogramme, unless the passenger or consignor has made, at the time when the package was handed over to the carrier, a special declaration of interest in delivery at destination and has paid a supplementary sum if the case so requires. In that case the carrier will be liable to pay a sum not exceeding the declared sum, unless he proves that the sum is greater than the passenger's or consignor's actual interest in delivery at destination.
   (b) In the case of loss, damage or delay of part of registered baggage or cargo, or of any object contained therein, the weight to be taken into consideration in determining the amount to which the carrier's liability is limited shall be only the total weight of the package or packages concerned. Nevertheless, when the loss, damage or delay of a part of the registered baggage or cargo, or of an object contained therein, affects the value of other packages covered by the same baggage check or the same air waybill, the total weight of such package or packages shall also be taken into consideration in determining the limit of liability.
3. As regards objects of which the passenger takes charge himself the liability of the carrier is limited to five thousand francs per passenger.
4. The limits prescribed in this Article shall not prevent the court from awarding, in accordance with its own law, in addition, the whole or part of the court costs and of the other expenses of the litigation incurred by the plaintiff. The foregoing provision shall not apply if the amount of the damages awarded, excluding court costs and other expenses of litigation, does not exceed the sum which the carrier has offered in writing to the plaintiff within a period of six months from the date of the occurrence causing the damage, or before the commencement of the action, if that is later.
5. The sums mentioned in francs in this Article shall be deemed to refer to a currency unit consisting of sixty-five and a half milligrammes of gold of millesimal fineness nine hundred. These sums may be converted into national currencies in round figures. Conversion of the sums into national currencies other than gold

shall, in case of judicial proceedings, be made according to the gold value of such currencies at the date of the judgment.

Article 23

1. Any provision tending to relieve the carrier of liability or to fix a lower limit than that which is laid down in this Convention shall be null and void, but the nullity of any such provision does not involve the nullity of the whole contract, which shall remain subject to the provisions of this Convention.
2. Paragraph 1 of this Article shall not apply to provisions governing loss or damage resulting from the inherent defect, quality or vice of the cargo carried.

Article 24

1. In the cases covered by Articles 18 and 19 any action for damages, however founded, can only be brought subject to the conditions and limits set out in this Convention.
2. In the cases covered by Article 17 the provisions of the preceding paragraph also apply, without prejudice to the questions as to who are the persons who have the right to bring suit and what are their respective rights.

Article 25 The limits of liability specified in Article 22 shall not apply if it is proved that the damage resulted from an act or omission of the carrier, his servants or agents, done with intent to cause damage or recklessly and with knowledge that damage would probably result; provided that, in the case of such act or omission of a servant or agent, it is also proved that he was acting within the scope of his employment.

Article 25 A

1. If an action is brought against a servant or agent of the carrier arising out of damage to which this Convention relates, such servant or agent, if he proves that he acted within the scope of his employment, shall be entitled to avail himself of the limits of liability which that carrier himself is entitled to invoke under Article 22.
2. The aggregate of the amounts recoverable from the carrier, his servants and agents, in that case, shall not exceed the said limits.
3. The provisions of paragraphs 1 and 2 of this Article shall not apply if it is proved that the damage resulted from an act or omission of the servant or agent done with intent to cause damage or recklessly and with knowledge that damage would probably result.

Article 26

1. Receipt by the person entitled to delivery of baggage or cargo without complaint is prima facie evidence that the same has been delivered in good condition and in accordance with the document of carriage.
2. In the case of damage, the person entitled to delivery must complain to the carrier forthwith after the discovery of the damage, and, at the latest, within seven days from the date of receipt in the case of baggage and fourteen days from the date of receipt in the case of cargo. In the case of delay the complaint must be made

at the latest within twenty-one days from the date on which the baggage or cargo have been placed at his disposal.

3. Every complaint must be made in writing upon the document of carriage or by separate notice in writing despatched within the times aforesaid.
4. Failing complaint within the times aforesaid, no action shall lie against the carrier, save in the case of fraud on his part.

Article 27 In the case of the death of the person liable, an action for damages lies in accordance with the terms of this Convention against those legally representing his estate.

Article 28

1. An action for damages must be brought, at the option of the plaintiff, in the territory of one of the High Contracting Parties, either before the Court having jurisdiction where the carrier is ordinarily resident, or has his principal place of business, or has an establishment by which the contract has been made or before the Court having jurisdiction at the place of destination.
2. Questions of procedure shall be governed by the law of the Court seized of the case.

Article 29

1. The right to damages shall be extinguished if an action is not brought within two years, reckoned from the date of arrival at the destination, or from the date on which the aircraft ought to have arrived, or from the date on which the carriage stopped.
2. The method of calculating the period of limitation shall be determined by the law of the Court seized of the case.

Article 30

1. In the case of carriage to be performed by various successive carriers and falling within the definition set out in the third paragraph of Article 1, each carrier who accepts passengers, baggage or cargo is subjected to the rules set out in this Convention and is deemed to be one of the contracting parties to the contract of carriage in so far as the contract deals with that part of the carriage which is performed under his supervision.
2. In the case of carriage of this nature, the passenger or his representative can take action only against the carrier who performed the carriage during which the accident or the delay occurred, save in the case where, by express agreement, the first carrier has assumed liability for the whole journey.
3. As regards baggage or cargo, the passenger or consignor will have a right of action against the first carrier, and the passenger or consignee who is entitled to delivery will have a right of action against the last carrier, and further, each may take action against the carrier who performed the carriage during which the destruction, loss, or damage or delay took place. These carriers will be jointly and severally liable to the passenger or to the consignor or consignee.

Chapter IV – Provisions Relating to Combined Carriage

Article 31

1. In the case of combined carriage performed partly by air and partly by any other mode of carriage, the provisions of this Convention apply only to the carriage by air, provided that the carriage by air falls within the terms of Article 1.
2. Nothing in this Convention shall prevent the parties in the case of combined carriage from inserting in the document of air carriage conditions relating to other modes of carriage, provided that the provisions of this Convention are observed as regards the carriage by air.

Chapter V – General and Final Provisions

Article 32 Any clause contained in the contract and all special agreements entered into before the damage occurred by which the parties purport to infringe the rules laid down by this Convention, whether by deciding the law to be applied, or by altering the rules as to jurisdiction shall be null and void. Nevertheless, for the carriage of cargo arbitration clauses are allowed, subject to this Convention, if the arbitration is to take place within one of the jurisdictions referred to in the first paragraph of Article 28.

Article 33 Nothing contained in this Convention shall prevent the carrier either from refusing to enter into any contract of carriage, or from making regulations which do not conflict with the provisions of this Convention.

Article 34 The provisions of Articles 3 to 9 inclusive relating to documents of carriage shall not apply in the case of carriage performed in extraordinary circumstances outside the normal scope of an air carrier's business.

Article 35 The expression 'days' when used in this Convention means current days not working days.

Article 36 DELETED FOR PURPOSES OF THIS BOOK

Article 40 A

1. In Article 37, paragraph 2 and Article 40, paragraph 1, the expression High Contracting Party shall mean State. In all other cases, the expression High Contracting Party shall mean a State whose ratification of or adherence to the Convention has become effective and whose denunciation thereof has not become effective.
2. DELETED FOR PURPOSES OF THIS BOOK

Article 41 DELETED FOR PURPOSES OF THIS BOOK
Additional Protocol
DELETED FOR PURPOSES OF THIS BOOK

Warsaw [unamended]

International Carriage under the Unamended Warsaw Convention

CHAPTER I Scope—Definitions

Article 1

(1) This Schedule applies to all international carriage of persons, baggage or cargo performed by aircraft for reward. It applies equally to gratuitous carriage by aircraft performed by an air transport undertaking.

(2) 'International carriage' means any carriage in which, according to the contract made by the parties, the place of departure and the place of destination, whether or not there be a break in the carriage or a transhipment, are situated either within the territories of two States Parties to the Convention for the Unification of Certain Rules relating to the International Carriage by Air signed at Warsaw on behalf of His Majesty on 12th October 1929, or within the territory of a single such State, if there is an agreed stopping place within the territory subject to the sovereignty, suzerainty, mandate or authority of another State, even though that State is not a party to the said Convention of 1929.

(3) A carriage to be performed by several successive air carriers is deemed, for the purposes of this Schedule, to be one undivided carriage, if it has been regarded by the parties as a single operation, whether it had been agreed upon under the form of a single contract or of a series of contracts, and it does not lose its international character merely because one contract of a series of contracts is to be performed entirely within a territory subject to the sovereignty, suzerainty, mandate or authority of the same High Contracting Party.

Article 2

(1) This Schedule applies to carriage performed by the State, not being a State which has availed itself of the Additional Protocol to the Warsaw Convention, or by legally constituted public bodies, provided it falls within the conditions laid down in Article 1.

(2) This Schedule does not apply to carriage performed under the terms of any international postal Convention.

CHAPTER II Documents of Carriage

SECTION 1—PASSENGER, TICKET

Article 3 DELETED FOR THE PURPOSES OF THIS BOOK
SECTION 2—BAGGAGE CHECK

Article 4 DELETED FOR THE PURPOSES OF THIS BOOK
SECTION 3—AIR WAYBILL

Article 5

(1) Every carrier of cargo has the right to require the consignor to make out and hand over to him a document called an 'air waybill'; every consignor has the right to require the carrier to accept this document.

(2) The absence, irregularity or loss of this document does not affect the existence of the validity of the contract of carriage which shall, subject to the provisions of Article 9, be none the less governed by the rules of this Schedule.

Article 6

(1) The air waybill shall be made out by the consignor in three original parts and be handed over with the cargo.

(2) The first part shall be marked 'for the carrier' and shall be signed by the consignor. The second part shall be marked 'for the consignee'; it shall be signed by the consignor and by the carrier and shall accompany the cargo. The third part shall be signed by the carrier and handed by him to the consignor after the cargo has been accepted.

(3) The carrier shall sign on acceptance of the cargo.

(4) The signature of the carrier may be stamped; that of the consignor may be printed or stamped.

(5) If, at the request of the consignor, the carrier makes out the air waybill, he shall be deemed, subject to proof to the contrary, to have done so on behalf of the consignor.

Article 7 The carrier of cargo has the right to require the consignor to make out separate air waybills when there is more than one package.

Article 8 The air waybill shall contain the following particulars: —

(a) the place and date of its execution;
(b) the place of departure and of destination;
(c) the agreed stopping places, provided that the carrier may reserve the right to alter the stopping places in case of necessity, and that if he exercises that right the alteration shall not have the effect of depriving the carriage of its international character;
(d) the name and address of the consignor;
(e) the name and address of the first carrier;
(f) the name and address of the consignee, if the case so requires;
(g) the nature of the cargo;
(h) the number of the packages, the method of packing and the particular marks or numbers upon them;
(i) the weight, the quantity and the volume or dimensions of the cargo;
(j) the apparent condition of the cargo and of the packing;
(k) the freight, if it has been agreed upon, the date and place of payment, and the person who is to pay it;
(l) if the cargo is sent for payment on delivery, the price of the cargo, and, if the case so requires, the amount of the expenses incurred;
(m) the amount of the value declared in accordance with Article 22(2);

(n) the number of parts of the air waybill;
(o) the documents handed to the carrier to accompany the air waybill;
(p) the time fixed for the completion of the carriage and a brief note of the route to be followed, if these matters have been agreed upon;
(q) a statement that the carriage is subject to the rules relating to liability established by the Warsaw Convention.

Article 9 If the carrier accepts cargo without an air waybill having been made out, or if the air waybill does not contain all the particulars set out in Article 8 (a) to (i) inclusive and (q), the carrier shall not be entitled to avail himself of the provisions of this Schedule which exclude or limit his liability.

Article 10

(1) The consignor is responsible for the correctness of the particulars and statements relating to the cargo which he inserts in the air waybill.
(2) The consignor will be liable for all damage suffered by the carrier or any other person by reason of the irregularity, incorrectness or incompleteness of the said particulars and statements.

Article 11

(1) The air waybill is prima facie evidence of the conclusion of the contract, of the receipt of the cargo and of the conditions of carriage.
(2) The statements in the air waybill relating to the weight, dimensions and packing of the cargo, as well as those relating to the number of packages, are prima facie evidence of the facts stated; those relating to the quantity, volume and condition of the cargo do not constitute evidence against the carrier except so far as they both have been and are stated in the air waybill to have been, checked by him in the presence of the consignor, or relate to the apparent condition of the cargo.

Article 12

(1) Subject to his liability to carry out all his obligations under the contract of carriage, the consignor has the right to dispose of the cargo by withdrawing it at the aerodrome of departure or destination, or by stopping it in the course of the journey on any landing, or by calling for it to be delivered at the place of destination or in the course of the journey to a person other than the consignee named in the air waybill, or by requiring it to be returned to the aerodrome of departure. He must not exercise this right of disposition in such a way as to prejudice the carrier or other consignors and he must repay any expenses occasioned by the exercise of this right.
(2) If it is impossible to carry out the orders of the consignor the carrier must so inform him forthwith.
(3) If the carrier obeys the orders of the consignor for the disposition of the cargo without requiring the production of the part of the air waybill delivered to the latter, he will be liable, without prejudice to his right of recovery from the consignor,

for any damage which may be caused thereby to any person who is lawfully in possession of that part of the air waybill.

(4) The right conferred on the consignor ceases at the moment when that of the consignee begins in accordance with Article 13. Nevertheless, if the consignee declines to accept the waybill or the cargo, or if he cannot be communicated with, the consignor resumes his right of disposition.

Article 13

(1) Except in the circumstances set out in the preceding Article, the consignee is entitled, on arrival of the cargo at the place of destination, to require the carrier to hand over to him the air waybill and to deliver the cargo to him, on payment of the charges due and on complying with the conditions of carriage set out in the air waybill.

(2) Unless it is otherwise agreed, it is the duty of the carrier to give notice to the consignee as soon as the cargo arrives.

(3) If the carrier admits the loss of the cargo, or if the cargo has not arrived at the expiration of seven days after the date on which it ought to have arrived, the consignee is entitled to put into force against the carrier the rights which flow from the contract of carriage.

Article 14 The consignor and the consignee can respectively enforce all the rights given them by Articles 12 and 13, each in his own name, whether he is acting in his own interest or in the interest of another, provided that he carries out the obligations imposed by the contract.

Article 15

(1) Articles 12, 13 and 14 do not affect either the relations of the consignor or the consignee with each other or the mutual relations of third parties whose rights are derived either from the consignor or from the consignee.

(2) The provisions of Articles 12, 13 and 14 can only be varied by express provision in the air waybill.

Article 16

(1) The consignor must furnish such information and attach to the air waybill such documents as are necessary to meet the formalities of customs, octroi or police before the cargo can be delivered to the consignee. The consignor is liable to the carrier for any damage occasioned by the absence, insufficiency or irregularity of any such information or documents, unless the damage is due to the fault of the carrier or his servants or agents.

(2) The carrier is under no obligation to enquire into the correctness or sufficiency of such information or documents.

CHAPTER III Liability of the Carrier

Article 17 DELETED FOR THE PURPOSES OF THIS BOOK

Article 18

(1) The carrier is liable for damage sustained in the event of the destruction or loss of, or damage to, any registered baggage or any cargo, if the occurrence which caused the damage so sustained took place during the carriage by air.

(2) The carriage by air within the meaning of the preceding paragraph comprises the period during which the baggage or cargo is in the charge of the carrier, whether in an aerodrome or on board an aircraft, or, in the case of a landing outside an aerodrome in any place whatsoever.

(3) The period of carriage by air does not extend to any carriage by land, by sea or by river performed outside an aerodrome. If, however, such a carriage takes place in the performance of a contract for carriage by air, for the purpose of loading, delivery or transhipment, any damage is presumed, subject to proof to the contrary, to have been the result of an event which took place during the carriage by air.

Article 19 The carrier is liable for damage occasioned by delay in the carriage by air of passengers, baggage or cargo.

Article 20

(1) The carrier is not liable if he proves that he and his servants or agents have taken all necessary measures to avoid the damage or that it was impossible for him or them to take such measures.

(2) In the carriage of cargo and baggage the carrier is not liable if he proves that the damage was occasioned by negligent pilotage or negligence in the handling of the aircraft or in navigation and that, in all other respects, he and his servants or agents have taken all necessary measures to avoid the damage.

Article 21 If the carrier proves that the damage was caused by or contributed to by the negligence of the injured person the court may, in accordance with the provisions of its own law, exonerate the carrier wholly or partly from his liability.

Article 22

(1) DELETED FOR THE PURPOSES OF THIS BOOK [passenger]

(2) In the carriage of registered baggage and of cargo, the liability of the carrier is limited to a sum of 250 francs per kilogramme, unless the consignor has made, at the time when the package was handed over to the carrier, a special declaration of the value at delivery and has paid a supplementary sum if the case so requires. In that case the carrier will be liable to pay a sum not exceeding the declared sum, unless he proves that the sum is greater than the actual value to the consignor at delivery.

(3) As regards objects of which the passenger takes charge himself the liability of the carrier is limited to 5,000 francs per passenger.

(4) The sums mentioned above shall be deemed to refer to the French franc consisting of 65½ milligrammes gold of millesimal fineness 900. These sums may be converted into any national currency in round figures.

Article 23 Any provision tending to relieve the carrier of liability or to fix a lower limit than that which is laid down in this Schedule shall be null and void, but the nullity of any such provision does not involve the nullity of the whole contract, which shall remain subject to the provisions of this Schedule.

Article 24

(1) In the cases covered by Articles 18 and 19 any action for damages, however founded, can only be brought subject to the conditions and limits set out in this Schedule.

(2) In the cases covered by Article 17 the provisions of the preceding paragraph also apply without prejudice to the questions as to who are the persons who have the right to bring suit and what are their respective rights.

Article 25

(1) The carrier shall not be entitled to avail himself of the provisions of this Schedule which exclude or limit his liability, if the damage is caused by his wilful misconduct, or by such default on his part as, in accordance with the law of the court seized of the case, is considered to be equivalent to wilful misconduct.

(2) Similarly, the carrier shall not be entitled to avail himself of the said provisions if the damage is caused as aforesaid by any servant or agent of the carrier acting within the scope of his employment.

Article 26

(1) Receipt by the person entitled to delivery of baggage or cargo without complaint is prima facie evidence that the same has been delivered in good condition and in accordance with the document of carriage.

(2) In the case of damage, the person entitled to delivery must complain to the carrier forthwith after the discovery of the damage, and, at the latest, within three days from the date of receipt in the case of baggage and seven days from the date of receipt in the case of cargo. In the case of delay the complaint must be made at the latest within fourteen days from the date on which the baggage or cargo has been placed at his disposal.

(3) Every complaint must be made in writing upon the document of carriage or by separate notice in writing despatched within the times aforesaid.

(4) Failing complaint within the times aforesaid, no action shall lie against the carrier, save in the case of fraud on his part.

Article 27 In the case of the death of the person liable, an action for damages lies in accordance with the terms of this Schedule against those legally representing his estate.

Article 28

(1) An action for damages must be brought, at the option of the plaintiff, in the territory of one of the High Contracting Parties to the Warsaw Convention, either before the court having jurisdiction where the carrier is ordinarily resident, or has his principal place of business, or has an establishment by which the contract has been made or before the court having jurisdiction at the place of destination.

(2) Questions of procedure shall be governed by the law of the court seized of the case.

Article 29

(1) The right to damages shall be extinguished if an action is not brought within two years, reckoned from the date of arrival at the destination, or from the date on which the aircraft ought to have arrived, or from the date on which the carriage stopped.

(2) The method of calculating the period of limitation shall be determined by the law of the court seized of the case.

Article 30

(1) In the case of carriage to be performed by various successive carriers and falling within the definition set out in the third paragraph of Article 1, each carrier who accepts passengers, baggage or cargo is subjected to the rules set out in this Schedule and is deemed to be one of the contracting parties to the contract of carriage in so far as the contract deals with that part of the carriage which is performed under his supervision.

(2) In the case of carriage of this nature, the passenger or his representative can take action only against the carrier who performed the carriage during which the accident or the delay occurred, save in the case where, by express agreement, the first carrier has assumed liability for the whole journey.

(3) As regards baggage or cargo, the passenger or consignor will have a right of action against the first carrier, and the passenger or consignee who is entitled to delivery will have a right of action against the last carrier, and further, each may take action against the carrier who performed the carriage during which the destruction, loss, damage or delay took place. These carriers will be jointly and severally liable to the passenger or to the consignor or consignee.

CHAPTER IV Provisions Relating to Combined Carriage

Article 31

(1) In the case of combined carriage performed partly by air and partly by any other mode of carriage, the provisions of this Schedule apply to the carriage by air, provided that the carriage by air falls within the terms of Article 1.

(2) Nothing in this Schedule shall prevent the parties in the case of combined carriage from inserting in the document of air carriage conditions relating to other modes of carriage, provided that the provisions of this Schedule are observed as regards the carriage by air.

CHAPTER V General and Final Provisions

Article 32 Any clause contained in the contract and all special agreements entered into before the damage occurred by which the parties purport to infringe the rules laid down by this Schedule, whether by deciding the law to be applied, or by altering the rules as to jurisdiction, shall be null and void. Nevertheless, for the carriage of cargo arbitration clauses are allowed, subject to this Schedule, if the arbitration is to take place within one of the jurisdictions referred to in the first paragraph of Article 28.

Article 33 Nothing contained in this Schedule shall prevent the carrier either from refusing to enter into any contract of carriage, or from making regulations which do not conflict with the provisions of this Schedule.

Article 34 This Schedule does not apply to international carriage by air performed by way of experimental trial by air navigation undertakings with the view to the establishment of a regular line of air navigation, nor does it apply to carriage performed in extraordinary circumstances outside the normal scope of an air carrier's business.

Article 35 The expression 'days' when used in this Schedule means current days not working days.

ADDITIONAL PROTOCOL TO THE WARSAW CONVENTION

DELETED FOR THE PURPOSES OF THIS BOOK

IATA 600b Air Waybill Conditions

RESOLUTION 600b – AIR WAYBILL – CONDITIONS OF CONTRACT

I. NOTICE APPEARING ON THE FACE OF THE AIR WAYBILL

It is agreed that the goods described herein are accepted in apparent good order and condition (except as noted) for carriage

SUBJECT TO THE CONDITIONS OF CONTRACT ON THE REVERSE HEREOF. ALL GOODS MAY BE CARRIED BY ANY OTHER MEANS INCLUDING ROAD OR ANY OTHER CARRIER UNLESS SPECIFIC CONTRARY INSTRUCTIONS ARE GIVEN HEREON BY THE SHIPPER, AND SHIPPER AGREES THAT THE SHIPMENT MAY BE CARRIED VIA INTERMEDIATE STOPPING PLACES WHICH THE CARRIER DEEMS APPPROPRIATE. THE SHIPPER'S ATTENTION IS DRAWN TO THE NOTICE CONCERNING CARRIER'S LIMITATION OF LIABILITY. Shipper may increase such limitation of liability by declaring a higher value for carriage and paying supplemental charge if required.

II. CONDITIONS OF CONTRACT ON REVERSE SIDE OF THE AIR WAYBILL

NOTICE CONCERNING CARRIERS' LIMITATION OF LIABILITY

If the carriage involves an ultimate destination or stop in a country other than the country of departure, the Warsaw Convention or the Montreal Convention may be applicable and in most cases limit the liability of the Carrier in respect of loss of, damage or delay to cargo. Depending on the applicable regime, and unless a higher value is declared, liability of the Carrier may be limited to 17 Special Drawing Rights per kilogram or 250 French gold francs per kilogram, converted into national currency under applicable law. Carrier will treat 250 French gold francs to be the conversion equivalent of 17 Special Drawing Rights unless a greater amount is specified in the Carrier's conditions of carriage.

* This Resolution is in the hands of all IATA Cargo Agents.

CONDITIONS OF CONTRACT

1. In this contract and the Notices appearing hereon:

CARRIER includes the air carrier issuing this air waybill and all carriers that carry or undertake to carry the cargo or perform any other services related to such carriage.

SPECIAL DRAWING RIGHT (SDR) is a Special Drawing Right as defined by the International Monetary Fund.

WARSAW CONVENTION means whichever of the following instruments is applicable to the contract of carriage:

the Convention for the Unification of Certain Rules Relating to International Carriage by Air, signed at Warsaw, 12 October 1929;

that Convention as amended at The Hague on 28 September 1955; that Convention as amended at The Hague 1955 and by Montreal Protocol No. 1, 2, or 4 (1975) as the case may be.

MONTREAL CONVENTION means the Convention for the Unification of Certain Rules for International Carriage by Air, done at Montreal on 28 May 1999.

2./2.1 Carriage is subject to the rules relating to liability established by the Warsaw Convention or the Montreal Convention unless such carriage is not 'international carriage' as defined by the applicable Conventions.

2.2 To the extent not in conflict with the foregoing, carriage and other related services performed by each Carrier are subject to:

2.2.1 applicable laws and government regulations;

2.2.2 provisions contained in the air waybill, Carrier's conditions of carriage and related rules, regulations, and timetables (but not the times of departure and arrival stated therein) and applicable tariffs of such Carrier, which are made part hereof, and which may be inspected at any airports or other cargo sales offices from which it operates regular services. When carriage is to/from the USA, the shipper and the consignee are entitled, upon request, to receive a free copy of the Carrier's conditions of carriage. The Carrier's conditions of carriage include, but are not limited to:

2.2.2.1 limits on the Carrier's liability for loss, damage or delay of goods, including fragile or perishable goods;

2.2.2.2 claims restrictions, including time periods within which shippers or consignees must file a claim or bring an action against the Carrier for its acts or omissions, or those of its agents;

2.2.2.3 rights, if any, of the Carrier to change the terms of the contract;

2.2.2.4 rules about Carrier's right to refuse to carry;

2.2.2.5 rights of the Carrier and limitations concerning delay or failure to perform service, including schedule changes, substitution of alternate Carrier or aircraft and rerouting.

3. The agreed stopping places (which may be altered by Carrier in case of necessity) are those places, except the place of departure and place of destination, set forth on the face hereof or shown in Carrier's timetables as scheduled stopping places for the route. Carriage to be performed hereunder by several successive Carriers is regarded as a single operation.

4. For carriage to which neither the Warsaw Convention nor the Montreal Convention applies, Carrier's liability limitation shall not be less than the per kilogram monetary limit set out in Carrier's tariffs or general conditions of carriage for cargo lost, damaged or delayed, provided that any such limitation of liability in an amount less than 17 SDR per kilogram will not apply for carriage to or from the United States.

5./5.1 Except when the Carrier has extended credit to the consignee without the written consent of the shipper, the shipper guarantees payment of all charges for the carriage due in accordance with Carrier's tariff, conditions of carriage and related regulations, applicable laws (including national laws implementing the Warsaw Convention and the Montreal Convention), government regulations, orders and requirements.

5.2 When no part of the consignment is delivered, a claim with respect to such consignment will be considered even though transportation charges thereon are unpaid.

6./6.1 For cargo accepted for carriage, the Warsaw Convention and the Montreal Convention permit shipper to increase the limitation of liability by declaring a higher value for carriage and paying a supplemental charge if required.

6.2 In carriage to which neither the Warsaw Convention nor the Montreal Convention applies Carrier shall, in accordance with the procedures set forth in its general conditions of carriage and applicable tariffs, permit shipper to increase the limitation of liability by declaring a higher value for carriage and paying a supplemental charge if so required.

7./7.1 In cases of loss of, damage or delay to part of the cargo, the weight to be taken into account in determining Carrier's limit of liability shall be only the weight of the package or packages concerned.

7.2 Notwithstanding any other provisions, for 'foreign air transportation' as defined by the U.S. Transportation Code:

7.2.1 in the case of loss of, damage or delay to a shipment, the weight to be used in determining Carrier's limit of liability shall be the weight which is used to determine the charge for carriage of such shipment; and

7.2.2 in the case of loss of, damage or delay to a part of a shipment, the shipment weight in 7.2.1 shall be prorated to the packages covered by the same air waybill whose value is affected by the loss, damage or delay. The weight applicable in the case of loss or damage to one or more articles in a package shall be the weight of the entire package.

8. Any exclusion or limitation of liability applicable to Carrier shall apply to Carrier's agents, employees, and representatives and to any person whose aircraft or equipment is used by Carrier for carriage and such person's agents, employees and representatives.

9. Carrier undertakes to complete the carriage with reasonable dispatch. Where permitted by applicable laws, tariffs and government regulations, Carrier may use alternative carriers, aircraft or modes of transport without notice but with due regard to the interests of the shipper. Carrier is authorised by the shipper to select the routing and all intermediate stopping places that it deems appropriate or to change or deviate from the routing shown on the face hereof.

10. Receipt by the person entitled to delivery of the cargo without complaint shall be prima facie evidence that the cargo has been delivered in good condition and in accordance with the contract of carriage.

10.1 In the case of loss of, damage or delay to cargo a written complaint must be made to Carrier by the person entitled to delivery. Such complaint must be made:

10.1.1 in the case of damage to the cargo, immediately after discovery of the damage and at the latest within 14 days from the date of receipt of the cargo;

10.1.2 in the case of delay, within 21 days from the date on which the cargo was placed at the disposal of the person entitled to delivery.

10.1.3 in the case of non-delivery of the cargo, within 120 days from the date of issue of the air waybill, or if an air waybill has not been issued, within 120 days from the date of receipt of the cargo for transportation by the Carrier.

10.2 Such complaint may be made to the Carrier whose air waybill was used, or to the first Carrier or to the last Carrier or to the Carrier, which performed the carriage during which the loss, damage or delay took place.

10.3 Unless a written complaint is made within the time limits specified in 10.1 no action may be brought against Carrier.

10.4 Any rights to damages against Carrier shall be extinguished unless an action is brought within two years from the date of arrival at the destination, or from the date on which the aircraft ought to have arrived, or from the date on which the carriage stopped.

11. Shipper shall comply with all applicable laws and government regulations of any country to or from which the cargo may be carried, including those relating to the packing, carriage or delivery of the cargo, and shall furnish such information and attach such documents to the air waybill as may be necessary to comply with such laws and regulations. Carrier is not liable to shipper and shipper shall indemnify Carrier for loss or expense due to shipper's failure to comply with this provision.
12. No agent, employee or representative of Carrier has authority to alter, modify or waive any provisions of this contract.

Ocean

Hague

International Convention for the Unification of Certain Rules of Law relating to Bills of Lading ('Hague Rules'), and Protocol of Signature (Brussels, 25 August 1924)

DELETED FOR THE PURPOSES OF THIS BOOK [List all the Heads of States who were originally party to this Convention]

HAVING RECOGNIZED the utility of fixing by agreement certain uniform rules of law relating to bills of lading,

HAVE DECIDED to conclude a convention with this object and have appointed the following Plenipotentiaries:

WHO, duly authorized thereto, have agreed as follows:

Article 1

In this Convention the following words are employed with the meanings set out below:

(a) 'Carrier' includes the owner or the charterer who enters into a contract of carriage with a shipper.
(b) 'Contract of carriage' applies only to contracts of carriage covered by a bill of lading or any similar document of title, in so far as such document relates to the carriage of goods by sea, including any bill of lading or any similar document as aforesaid issued under or pursuant to a charter party from the moment at which such bill of lading or similar document of title regulates the relations between a carrier and a holder of the same.
(c) 'Goods' includes goods, wares, merchandise and articles of every kind whatsoever except live animals and cargo which by the contract of carriage in stated as being carried on deck and is so carried.
(d) 'Ship' means any vessel used for the carriage of goods by sea.
(e) 'Carriage of goods' covers the period from the time when the goods are loaded on to the time they are discharged from the ship.

Article 2

Subject to the provisions of Article 6, under every contract of carriage of goods by sea the carrier, in relation to the loading, handling, stowage, carriage, custody, care and discharge of such goods, shall be subject to the responsibilities and liabilities, and entitled to the rights and immunities hereinafter set forth.

Article 3

1. The carrier shall be bound before and at the beginning of the voyage to exercise due diligence to:
   (a) Make the ship seaworthy.
   (b) Properly man, equip and supply the ship.
   (c) Make the holds, refrigerating and cool chambers, and all other parts of the ship in which goods are carried, fit and safe for their reception, carriage and preservation.

2. Subject to the provisions of Article 4, the carrier shall properly and carefully load, handle, stow, carry, keep, care for, and discharge the goods carried.
3. After receiving the goods into his charge the carrier or the master or agent of the carrier shall, on demand of the shipper, issue to the shipper a bill of lading showing among other things:
   (a) The leading marks necessary for identification of the goods as the same are furnished in writing by the shipper before the loading of such goods starts, provided such marks are stamped or otherwise shown clearly upon the goods if uncovered, or on the cases or coverings in which such goods are contained, in such a manner as should ordinarily remain legible until the end of the voyage.
   (b) Either the number of packages or pieces, or the quantity, or weight, as the case may be, as furnished in writing by the shipper.
   (c) The apparent order and condition of the goods.

   Provided that no carrier, master or agent of the carrier shall be bound to state or show in the bill of lading any marks, number, quantity, or weight which he has reasonable ground for suspecting not accurately to represent the goods actually received, or which he has had no reasonable means of checking.
4. Such a bill of lading shall be prima facie evidence of the receipt by the carrier of the goods as therein described in accordance with paragraph 3(a), (b) and (c).
5. The shipper shall be deemed to have guaranteed to the carrier the accuracy at the time of shipment of the marks, number, quantity and weight, as furnished by him, and the shipper shall indemnity the carrier against all loss, damages and expenses arising or resulting from inaccuracies in such particulars. The right of the carrier to such indemnity shall in no way limit his responsibility and liability under the contract of carriage to any person other than the shipper.
6. Unless notice of loss or damage and the general nature of such loss or damage be given in writing to the carrier or his agent at the port of discharge before or at the time of the removal of the goods into the custody of the person entitled to delivery thereof under the contract of carriage, or, if the loss or damage be not apparent, within three days, such removal shall be prima facie evidence of the delivery by the carrier of the goods as described in the bill of lading.

   If the loss or damage is not apparent, the notice must be given within three days of the delivery of the goods.

   The notice in writing need not be given if the state of the goods has, at the time of their receipt, been the subject of joint survey or inspection.

   In any event the carrier and the ship shall be discharged from all liability in respect of loss or damage unless suit is brought within one year after delivery of the goods or the date when the goods should have been delivered.

   In the case of any actual or apprehended loss or damage the carrier and the receiver shall give all reasonable facilities to each other for inspecting and tallying the goods.
7. After the goods are loaded the bill of lading to be issued by the carrier, master, or agent of the carrier, to the shipper shall, if the shipper so demands, be a 'shipped' bill of lading, provided that if the shipper shall have previously taken up any document of title to such goods, he shall surrender the same as against the issue

of the 'shipped' bill of lading, but at the option of the carrier such document of title may be noted at the port of shipment by the carrier, master, or agent with the name or names of the ship or ships upon which the goods have been shipped and the date or dates of shipment, and when so noted, if it shows the particulars mentioned in paragraph 3 of Article 3, shall for the purpose of this Article be deemed to constitute a 'shipped' bill of lading.

8. Any clause, covenant, or agreement in a contract of carriage relieving the carrier or the ship from liability for loss or damage to, or in connexion with, goods arising from negligence, fault, or failure in the duties and obligations provided in this Article or lessening such liability otherwise than as provided in this Convention, shall be null and void and of no effect. A benefit of insurance in favour of the carrier or similar clause shall be deemed to be a clause relieving the carrier from liability.

Article 4

1. Neither the carrier nor the ship shall be liable for loss or damage arising or resulting from unseaworthiness unless caused by want of due diligence on the part of the carrier to make the ship seaworthy and to secure that the ship is properly manned, equipped and supplied, and to make the holds, refrigerating and cool chambers and all other parts of the ship in which goods are carried fit and safe for their reception, carriage and preservation in accordance with the provisions of paragraph 1 of Article 3. Whenever loss or damage has resulted from unseaworthiness the burden of proving the exercise of due diligence shall be on the carrier or other person claiming exemption under this Article.
2. Neither the carrier nor the ship shall be responsible for loss or damage arising or resulting from:
   (a) Act, neglect, or default of the master, mariner, pilot, or the servants of the carrier in the navigation or in the management of the ship.
   (b) Fire, unless caused by the actual fault or privity of the carrier.
   (c) Perils, dangers and accidents of the sea or other navigable waters.
   (d) Act of God.
   (e) Act of war.
   (f) Act of public enemies.
   (g) Arrest or restraint or princes, rulers or people, or seizure under legal process.
   (h) Quarantine restrictions.
   (i) Act or omission of the shipper or owner of the goods, his agent or representative.
   (j) Strikes or lockouts or stoppage or restraint of labour from whatever cause, whether partial or general.
   (k) Riots and civil commotions.
   (l) Saving or attempting to save life or property at sea.
   (m) Wastage in bulk or weight or any other loss or damage arising from inherent defect, quality or vice of the goods.
   (n) Insufficiency of packing.
   (o) Insufficiency or inadequacy of marks.
   (p) Latent defects not discoverable by due diligence.

(q) Any other cause arising without the actual fault or privity of the carrier, or without the actual fault or neglect of the agents or servants of the carrier, but the burden of proof shall be on the person claiming the benefit of this exception to show that neither the actual fault or privity of the carrier nor the fault or neglect of the agents or servants of the carrier contributed to the loss or damage.

3. The shipper shall not be responsible for loss or damage sustained by the carrier or the ship arising or resulting from any cause without the act, fault or neglect of the shipper, his agents or his servants.
4. Any deviation in saving or attempting to save life or property at sea or any reasonable deviation shall not be deemed to be an infringement or breach of this Convention or of the contract of carriage, and the carrier shall not be liable for any loss or damage resulting therefrom.
5. Neither the carrier nor the ship shall in any event be or become liable for any loss or damage to or in connexion with goods in an amount exceeding 100 pounds sterling per package or unit, or the equivalent of that sum in other currency unless the nature and value of such goods have been declared by the shipper before shipment and inserted in the bill of lading.

   This declaration if embodied in the bill of lading shall be prima facie evidence but shall not be binding or conclusive on the carrier.

   By agreement between the carrier, master or agent of the carrier and the shipper another maximum amount than that mentioned in this paragraph may be fixed, provided that such maximum shall not be less than the figure above named.

   Neither the carrier nor the ship shall be responsible in any event for loss or damage to, or in connexion with, goods if the nature or value thereof has been knowingly misstated by the shipper in the bill of lading.
6. Goods of an inflammable, explosive or dangerous nature to the shipment whereof the carrier, master or agent of the carrier has not consented with knowledge of their nature and character, may at any time before discharge be landed at any place, or destroyed or rendered innocuous by the carrier without compensation and the shipper of such goods shall be liable for all damage and expenses directly or indirectly arising out of or resulting from such shipment. If any such goods shipped with such knowledge and consent shall become a danger to the ship or cargo, they may in like manner be landed at any place or destroyed or rendered innocuous by the carrier without liability on the part of the carrier except to general average, if any.

Article 5

A carrier shall be at liberty to surrender in whole or in part all or any of his rights and immunities or to increase any of his responsibilities and obligations under this Convention, provided such surrender or increase shall be embodied in the bill of lading issued to the shipper.

The provisions of this Convention shall not be applicable to charter parties, but if bills of lading are issued in the case of a ship under a charter party they shall comply with the terms of this Convention. Nothing in these rules shall be held to prevent the insertion in a bill of lading of any lawful provision regarding general average.

Article 6

Notwithstanding the provisions of the preceding Articles, a carrier, master or agent of the carrier and a shipper shall in regard to any particular goods be at liberty to enter into any agreement in any terms as to the responsibility and liability of the carrier for such goods, and as to the rights and immunities of the carrier in respect of such goods, or his obligation as to seaworthiness, so far as this stipulation is not contrary to public policy, or the care or diligence of his servants or agents in regard to the loading, handling, stowage, carriage, custody, care and discharge of the goods carried by sea, provided that in this case no bill of lading has been or shall be issued and that the terms agreed shall be embodied in a receipt which shall be a non-negotiable document and shall be marked as such.

Any agreement so entered into shall have full legal effect.

Provided that this Article shall not apply to ordinary commercial shipments made in the ordinary course of trade, but only to other shipments where the character or condition of the property to be carried or the circumstances, terms and conditions under which the carriage is to be performed are such as reasonably to justify a special agreement.

Article 7

Nothing herein contained shall prevent a carrier or a shipper from entering into any agreement, stipulation, condition, reservation or exemption as to the responsibility and liability of the carrier or the ship for the loss or damage to, or in connexion with, the custody and care and handling of goods prior to the loading on, and subsequent to, the discharge from the ship on which the goods are carried by sea.

Article 8

The provisions of this Convention shall not affect the rights and obligations of the carrier under any statute for the time being in force relating to the limitation of the liability of owners of sea-going vessels.

Article 9

The monetary units mentioned in this Convention are to be taken to be gold value.

Those contracting States in which the pound sterling is not a monetary unit reserve to themselves the right of translating the sums indicated in this Convention in terms of pound sterling into terms of their own monetary system in round figures.

The national laws may reserve to the debtor the right of discharging his debt in national currency according to the rate of exchange prevailing on the day of the arrival of the ship at the port of discharge of the goods concerned.

Article 10

The provisions of this Convention shall apply to all bills of lading issued in any of the contracting States.

Article 11 – 16

DELETED FOR THE PURPOSES OF THIS BOOK [deals with how the convention was to be ratified]

DONE at Brussels, in a single copy, August 25th, 1924.

Hague/Visby

The Hague-Visby Rules – The Hague Rules as Amended by the Brussels Protocol 1968
Article I
In these Rules the following words are employed, with the meanings set out below:

(a) 'Carrier' includes the owner or the charterer who enters into a contract of carriage with a shipper.
(b) 'Contract of carriage' applies only to contracts of carriage covered by a bill of lading or any similar document of title, in so far as such document relates to the carriage of goods by sea, including any bill of lading or any similar document as aforesaid issued under or pursuant to a charter party from the moment at which such bill of lading or similar document of title regulates the relations between a carrier and a holder of the same.
(c) 'Goods' includes goods, wares, merchandise, and articles of every kind whatsoever except live animals and cargo which by the contract of carriage is stated as being carried on deck and is so carried.
(d) 'Ship' means any vessel used for the carriage of goods by sea.
(e) 'Carriage of goods' covers the period from the time when the goods are loaded on to the time they are discharged from the ship.

Article II

Subject to the provisions of Article VI, under every contract of carriage of goods by sea the carrier, in relation to the loading, handling, stowage, carriage, custody, care and discharge of such goods, shall be subject to the responsibilities and liabilities and entitled to the rights and immunities hereinafter set forth.

Article III

1. The carrier shall be bound before and at the beginning of the voyage to exercise due diligence to:
   (a) Make the ship seaworthy;
   (b) Properly man, equip and supply the ship;
   (c) Make the holds, refrigerating and cool chambers, and all other parts of the ship in which goods are carried, fit and safe for their reception, carriage and preservation.
2. Subject to the provisions of Article IV, the carrier shall properly and carefully load, handle, stow, carry, keep, care for, and discharge the goods carried.
3. After receiving the goods into his charge the carrier or the master or agent of the carrier shall, on demand of the shipper, issue to the shipper a bill of lading showing among other things:
   (a) The leading marks necessary for identification of the goods as the same are furnished in writing by the shipper before the loading of such goods starts, provided such marks are stamped or otherwise shown clearly upon the goods if uncovered, or on the cases or coverings in which such goods are contained, in such a manner as should ordinarily remain legible until the end of the voyage.

(b) Either the number of packages or pieces, or the quantity, or weight, as the case may be, as furnished in writing by the shipper.

(c) The apparent order and condition of the goods.

Provided that no carrier, master or agent of the carrier shall be bound to state or show in the bill of lading any marks, number, quantity or weight which he has reasonable ground for suspecting not accurately to represent the goods actually received, or which he has had no reasonable means of checking.

4. Such a bill of lading shall be prima facie evidence of the receipt by the carrier of the goods as therein described in accordance with paragraph 3 (a), (b) and (c). However, proof to the contrary shall not be admissible when the bill of lading has been transferred to a third party acting in good faith.

5. The shipper shall be deemed to have guaranteed to the carrier the accuracy at the time of shipment of the marks, number, quantity and weight, as furnished by him, and the shipper shall indemnify the carrier against all loss, damages and expenses arising or resulting from inaccuracies in such particulars. The right of the carrier to such indemnity shall in no way limit his responsibility and liability under the contract of carriage to any person other than the shipper.

6. Unless notice of loss or damage and the general nature of such loss or damage be given in writing to the carrier or his agent at the port of discharge before or at the time of the removal of the goods into the custody of the person entitled to delivery thereof under the contract of carriage, or, if the loss or damage be not apparent, within three days, such removal shall be prima facie evidence of the delivery by the carrier of the goods as described in the bill of lading.

The notice in writing need not be given if the state of the goods has, at the time of their receipt, been the subject of joint survey or inspection.

Subject to paragraph 6bis the carrier and the ship shall in any event be discharged from all liability whatsoever in respect of the goods, unless suit is brought within one year of their delivery or of the date when they should have been delivered. This period, may however, be extended if the parties so agree after the cause of action has arisen.

In the case of any actual or apprehended loss or damage the carrier and the receiver shall give all reasonable facilities to each other for inspecting and tallying the goods.

6.bis. An action for indemnity against a third person may be brought even after the expiration of the year provided for in the preceding paragraph if brought within the time allowed by the law of the Court seized of the case. However, the time allowed shall be not less than three months, commencing from the day when the person bringing such action for indemnity has settled the claim or has been served with process in the action against himself.

7. After the goods are loaded the bill of lading to be issued by the carrier, master, or agent of the carrier, to the shipper shall, if the shipper so demands be a 'shipped' bill of lading, provided that if the shipper shall have previously taken up any document of title to such goods, he shall surrender the same as against the issue of the 'shipped' bill of lading, but at the option of the carrier such document of

title may be noted at the port of shipment by the carrier, master, or agent with the name or names of the ship or ships upon which the goods have been shipped and the date or dates of shipment, and when so noted, if it shows the particulars mentioned in paragraph 3 of Article III, shall for the purpose of this article be deemed to constitute a 'shipped' bill of lading.

8. Any clause, covenant, or agreement in a contract of carriage relieving the carrier or the ship from liability for loss or damage to, or in connection with, goods arising from negligence, fault, or failure in the duties and obligations provided in this article or lessening such liability otherwise than as provided in these Rules, shall be null and void and of no effect. A benefit of insurance in favour of the carrier or similar clause shall be deemed to be a clause relieving the carrier from liability.

Article IV

1. Neither the carrier nor the ship shall be liable for loss or damage arising or resulting from unseaworthiness unless caused by want of due diligence on the part of the carrier to make the ship seaworthy, and to secure that the ship is properly manned, equipped and supplied, and to make the holds, refrigerating and cool chambers and all other parts of the ship in which goods are carried fit and safe for their reception, carriage and preservation in accordance with the provisions of paragraph 1 of Article III. Whenever loss or damage has resulted from unseaworthiness the burden of proving the exercise of due diligence shall be on the carrier or other person claiming exemption under this article.
2. Neither the carrier nor the ship shall be responsible for loss or damage arising or resulting from:
   (a) Act, neglect, or default of the master, mariner, pilot, or the servants of the carrier in the navigation or in the management of the ship.
   (b) Fire, unless caused by the actual fault or privity of the carrier.
   (c) Perils, dangers and accidents of the sea or other navigable waters.
   (d) Act of God.
   (e) Act of war.
   (f) Act of public enemies.
   (g) Arrest or restraint of princes, rulers or people, or seizure under legal process.
   (h) Quarantine restrictions.
   (i) Act or omission of the shipper or owner of the goods, his agent or representative.
   (j) Strikes or lockouts or stoppage or restraint of labour from whatever cause, whether partial or general.
   (k) Riots and civil commotions.
   (l) Saving or attempting to save life or property at sea.
   (m) Wastage in bulk of weight or any other loss or damage arising from inherent defect, quality or vice of the goods.
   (n) Insufficiency of packing.
   (o) Insufficiency or inadequacy of marks.
   (p) Latent defects not discoverable by due diligence.

(q) Any other cause arising without the actual fault or privity of the carrier, or without the fault or neglect of the agents or servants of the carrier, but the burden of proof shall be on the person claiming the benefit of this exception to show that neither the actual fault or privity of the carrier nor the fault or neglect of the agents or servants of the carrier contributed to the loss or damage.

3. The shipper shall not be responsible for loss or damage sustained by the carrier or the ship arising or resulting from any cause without the act, fault or neglect of the shipper, his agents or his servants.

4. Any deviation in saving or attempting to save life or property at sea or any reasonable deviation shall not be deemed to be an infringement or breach of these Rules or of the contract of carriage, and the carrier shall not be liable for any loss or damage resulting therefrom.

5. (a) Unless the nature and value of such goods have been declared by the shipper before shipment and inserted in the bill of lading, neither the carrier nor the ship shall in any event be or become liable for any loss or damage to or in connection with the goods in an amount exceeding the equivalent of 666.67 units of account per package or unit or units of account per kilo of gross weight of the goods lost or damaged, whichever is the higher.

(b) The total amount recoverable shall be calculated by reference to the value of such goods at the place and time at which the goods are discharged from the ship in accordance with the contract or should have been so discharged.

The value of the goods shall be fixed according to the commodity exchange price, or, if there be no such price, according to the current market price, or, if there be no commodity exchange price or current market price, by reference to the normal value of goods of the same kind and quality.

(c) Where a Container, pallet or similar article of transport is used to consolidate goods, the number of packages or units enumerated in the bill of lading as packed in such article of transport shall be deemed the number of packages or units for the purpose of this paragraph as far as these packages or units are concerned. Except as aforesaid such article of transport shall be considered the package or unit.

(d) The unit of account mentioned in this Article is the special drawing right as defined by the International Monetary Fund. The amounts mentioned in Hague/Visby Art. 4 sub-paragraph (a) of this paragraph shall be converted into national currency on the basis of the value of that currency on a date to be determined by the law of the Court seized of the case.

(e) Neither the carrier nor the ship shall be entitled to the benefit of the limitation of liability provided for in this paragraph if it is proved that the damage resulted from an act or omission of the carrier done with intent to cause damage, or recklessly and with knowledge that damage would probably result.

(f) The declaration mentioned in sub-paragraph (a) of this paragraph, if embodied in the bill of lading, shall be prima facie evidence, but shall not be binding or conclusive on the carrier.

(g) By agreement between the carrier, master or agent of the carrier and the shipper other maximum amounts than those mentioned in sub-paragraph (a) of this paragraph may be fixed, provided that no maximum amount so fixed shall be less than the appropriate maximum mentioned in that sub-paragraph.

(h) Neither the carrier nor the ship shall be responsible in any event for loss or damage to, or in connection with, goods if the nature or value thereof has been knowingly mis-stated by the shipper in the bill of lading.

6. Goods of an inflammable, explosive or dangerous nature to the shipment whereof the carrier, master or agent of the carrier has not consented with knowledge of their nature and character, may at any time before discharge be landed at any place, or destroyed or rendered innocuous by the carrier without compensation and the shipper of such goods shall be liable for all damages and expenses directly or indirectly arising out of or resulting from such shipment. If any such goods shipped with such knowledge and consent shall become a danger to the ship or cargo, they may in like manner be landed at any place or destroyed or rendered innocuous by the carrier without liability on the part of the carrier except to general average, if any.

Article IV bis

1. The defences and limits of liability provided for in these Rules shall apply in any action against the carrier in respect of loss or damage to goods covered by a contract of carriage whether the action be founded in contract or in tort.
2. If such an action is brought against a servant or agent of the carrier (such servant or agent not being an independent contractor), such servant or agent shall be entitled to avail himself of the defences and limits of liability which the carrier is entitled to invoke under these Rules.
3. The aggregate of the amounts recoverable from the carrier, and such servants and agents, shall in no case exceed the limit provided for in these Rules.
4. Nevertheless, a servant or agent of the carrier shall not be entitled to avail himself of the provisions of this article, if it is proved that the damage resulted from an act or omission of the servant or agent done with intent to cause damage or recklessly and with knowledge that damage would probably result.

Article V

A carrier shall be at liberty to surrender in whole or in part all or any of his rights and immunities or to increase any of his responsibilities and obligations under these Rules, provided such surrender or increase shall be embodied in the bill of lading issued to the shipper. The provisions of these Rules shall not be applicable to charter parties, but if bills of lading are issued in the case of a ship under a charter party they shall comply with the terms of these Rules. Nothing in these Rules shall be held to prevent the insertion in a bill of lading of any lawful provision regarding general average.

Article VI

Notwithstanding the provisions of the preceding articles, a carrier, master or agent of the carrier and a shipper shall in regard to any particular goods be at liberty to enter into any agreement in any terms as to the responsibility and liability of the carrier for such goods, and as to the rights and immunities of the carrier in respect of such goods, or his obligation as to seaworthiness, so far as this stipulation is not contrary to public policy, or the care or diligence of his servants or agents in regard to the loading, handling, stowage, carriage, custody, care and discharge of the goods carried by sea, provided that in this case no bill of lading has been or shall be issued and that the terms agreed shall be embodied in a receipt which shall be a non-negotiable document and shall be marked as such.

An agreement so entered into shall have full legal effect.

Provided that this article shall not apply to ordinary commercial shipments made in the ordinary course of trade, but only to other shipments where the character or condition of the property to be carried or the circumstances, terms and conditions under which the carriage is to be performed are such as reasonably to justify a special agreement.

Article VII

Nothing herein contained shall prevent a carrier or a shipper from entering into any agreement, stipulation, condition, reservation or exemption as to the responsibility and liability of the carrier or the ship for the loss or damage to, or in connection with, the custody and care and handling of goods prior to the loading on, and subsequent to the discharge from, the ship on which the goods are carried by sea.

Article VIII

The provisions of these Rules shall not affect the rights and obligations of the carrier under any statute for the time being in force relating to the limitation of the liability of owners of sea-going vessels.

Article IX

These Rules shall not affect the provisions of any international Convention or national law governing liability for nuclear damage.

Article X

The provisions of these Rules shall apply to every bill of lading relating to the carriage of goods between ports in two different States if

(a) the bill of lading is issued in a contracting State, or
(b) the carriage is from a port in a contracting State, or
(c) the contract contained in or evidenced by the bill of lading provides that these Rules or legislation of any State giving effect to them are to govern the contract; whatever may be the nationality of the ship, the carrier, the shipper, the consignee, or any other interested person.

(The last two paragraphs of this Article are not reproduced. They require contracting States to apply the Rules to bills of lading mentioned in the Article and authorise them to apply the Rules to other bills of lading.)

(Article 11 to 16 of the International Convention for the unification of certain rules of law relating to bills of lading signed at Brussels on August 25, 1974 are not reproduced. They deal with the coming into force of the Convention, procedure for ratification, accession and denunciation, and the right to call for a fresh conference to consider amendments to the Rules contained in the Convention.)

Hamburg

United Nations Convention on the Carriage of Goods by Sea ('Hamburg Rules')

(Hamburg, 31 March 1978)

PREAMBLE

THE STATES PARTIES TO THIS CONVENTION, HAVING RECOGNIZED the desirability of determining by agreement certain rules relating to the carriage of goods by sea, HAVING DECIDED to conclude a convention for this purpose and have thereto agreed as follows:

PART I. GENERAL PROVISIONS

Article 1. Definitions In this Convention:

1. 'Carrier' means any person by whom or in whose name a contract of carriage of goods by sea has been concluded with a shipper.
2. 'Actual carrier' means any person to whom the performance of the carriage of the goods, or of part of the carriage, has been entrusted by the carrier, and includes any other person to whom such performance has been entrusted.
3. 'Shipper' means any person by whom or in whose name or on whose behalf a contract of carriage of goods by sea has been concluded with a carrier, or any person by whom or in whose name or on whose behalf the goods are actually delivered to the carrier in relation to the contract of carriage by sea.
4. 'Consignee' means the person entitled to take delivery of the goods.
5. 'Goods' includes live animals; where the goods are consolidated in a Container, pallet or similar article of transport or where they are packed, goods include such article of transport or packaging if supplied by the shipper.
6. 'Contract of carriage by sea' means any contract whereby the carrier undertakes against payment of freight to carry goods by sea from one port to another; however, a contract which involves carriage by sea and also carriage by some other means is deemed to be a contract of carriage by sea for the purposes of this Convention only in so far as it relates to the carriage by sea.
7. 'Bill of lading' means a document which evidences a contract of carriage by sea and the taking over or loading of the goods by the carrier, and by which the carrier undertakes to deliver the goods against surrender of the document. A provision in the document that the goods are to be delivered to the order of a named person, or to order, or to bearer, constitutes such an undertaking.
8. 'Writing' includes, inter alia, telegram and telex.

Article 2. Scope of application

1. The provisions of this Convention are applicable to all contracts of carriage by sea between two different States, if:
   (a) the port of loading as provided for in the contract of carriage by sea is located in a Contracting State, or
   (b) the port of discharge as provided for in the contract of carriage by sea is located in a Contracting State, or

(c) one of the optional ports of discharge provided for in the contract of carriage by sea is the actual port of discharge and such port is located in a Contracting State, or
(d) the bill of lading or other document evidencing the contract of carriage by sea is issued in a Contracting State, or
(e) the bill of lading or other document evidencing the contract of carriage by sea provides that the provisions of this Convention or the legislation of any State giving effect to them are to govern the contract.

2. The provisions of this Convention are applicable without regard to the nationality of the ship, the carrier, the actual carrier, the shipper, the consignee or any other interested person.
3. The provisions of this Convention are not applicable to charter-parties. However, where a bill of lading is issued pursuant to a charter-party, the provisions of the Convention apply to such a bill of lading if it governs the relation between the carrier and the holder of the bill of lading, not being the charterer.
4. If a contract provides for future carriage of goods in a series of shipments during an agreed period, the provisions of this Convention apply to each shipment. However, where a shipment is made under a charter-party, the provisions of paragraph 3 of this article apply.

Article 3. Interpretation of the Convention In the interpretation and application of the provisions of this Convention regard shall be had to its international character and to the need to promote uniformity.

PART II. LIABILITY OF THE CARRIER

Article 4. Period of responsibility

1. The responsibility of the carrier for the goods under this Convention covers the period during which the carrier is in charge of the goods at the port of loading, during the carriage and at the port of discharge.
2. For the purpose of paragraph 1 of this article, the carrier is deemed to be in charge of the goods
   (a) from the time he has taken over the goods from:
      (i) the shipper, or a person acting on his behalf; or
      (ii) an authority or other third party to whom, pursuant to law or regulations applicable at the port of loading, the goods must be handed over for shipment;
   (b) until the time he has delivered the goods:
      (i) by handing over the goods to the consignee; or
      (ii) in cases where the consignee does not receive the goods from the carrier, by placing them at the disposal of the consignee in accordance with the contract or with the law or with the usage of the particular trade, applicable at the port of discharge; or
      (iii) by handing over the goods to an authority or other third party to whom, pursuant to law or regulations applicable at the port of discharge, the goods must be handed over.

3. In paragraphs 1 and 2 of this article, reference to the carrier or to the consignee means, in addition to the carrier or the consignee, the servants or agents, respectively of the carrier or the consignee.

Article 5. Basis of liability

1. The carrier is liable for loss resulting from loss of or damage to the goods, as well as from delay in delivery, if the occurrence which caused the loss, damage or delay took place while the goods were in his charge as defined in article 4, unless the carrier proves that he, his servants or agents took all measures that could reasonably be required to avoid the occurrence and its consequences.
2. Delay in delivery occurs when the goods have not been delivered at the port of discharge provided for in the contract of carriage by sea within the time expressly agreed upon or, in the absence of such agreement, within the time which it would be reasonable to require of a diligent carrier, having regard to the circumstances of the case.
3. The person entitled to make a claim for the loss of goods may treat the goods as lost if they have not been delivered as required by article 4 within 60 consecutive days following the expiry of the time for delivery according to paragraph 2 of this article.
4. (a) The carrier is liable
   (i) for loss of or damage to the goods or delay in delivery caused by fire, if the claimant proves that the fire arose from fault or neglect on the part of the carrier, his servants or agents;
   (ii) for such loss, damage or delay in delivery which is proved by the claimant to have resulted from the fault or neglect of the carrier, his servants or agents in taking all measures that could reasonably be required to put out the fire and avoid or mitigate its consequences.

   (b) In case of fire on board the ship affecting the goods, if the claimant or the carrier so desires, a survey in accordance with shipping practices must be held into the cause and circumstances of the fire, and a copy of the surveyor's report shall be made available on demand to the carrier and the claimant.
5. With respect to live animals, the carrier is not liable for loss, damage or delay in delivery resulting from any special risks inherent in that kind of carriage. If the carrier proves that he has complied with any special instructions given to him by the shipper respecting the animals and that, in the circumstances of the case, the loss, damage or delay in delivery could be attributed to such risks, it is presumed that the loss, damage or delay in delivery was so caused, unless there is proof that all or a part of the loss, damage or delay in delivery resulted from fault or neglect on the part of the carrier, his servants or agents.
6. The carrier is not liable, except in general average, where loss, damage or delay in delivery resulted from measures to save life or from reasonable measures to save property at sea.
7. Where fault or neglect on the part of the carrier, his servants or agents combines with another cause to produce loss, damage or delay in delivery, the carrier is liable only to the extent that the loss, damage or delay in delivery is attributable

to such fault or neglect, provided that the carrier proves the amount of the loss, damage or delay in delivery not attributable thereto.

Article 6. Limits of liability

1. (a) The liability of the carrier for loss resulting from loss of or damage to goods according to the provisions of article 5 is limited to an amount equivalent to 835 units of account per package or other shipping unit or 2.5 units of account per kilogram of gross weight of the goods lost or damaged, whichever is the higher.
   (b) The liability of the carrier for delay in delivery according to the provisions of article 5 is limited to an amount equivalent to two and a half times the freight payable for the goods delayed, but not exceeding the total freight payable under the contract of carriage of goods by sea.
   (c) In no case shall the aggregate liability of the carrier, under both subparagraphs (a) and (b) of this paragraph, exceed the limitation which would be established under subparagraph (a) of this paragraph for total loss of the goods with respect to which such liability was incurred.
2. For the purpose of calculating which amount is the higher in accordance with paragraph 1 (a) of this article, the following rules apply:
   (a) Where a Container, pallet or similar article of transport is used to consolidate goods, the package or other shipping units enumerated in the bill of lading, if issued, or otherwise in any other document evidencing the contract of carriage by sea, as packed in such article of transport are deemed packages or shipping units. Except as aforesaid the goods in such article of transport are deemed one shipping unit.
   (b) In cases where the article of transport itself has been lost or damaged, that article of transport, if not owned or otherwise supplied by the carrier, is considered one separate shipping unit.
3. Unit of account means the unit of account mentioned in article 26.
4. By agreement between the carrier and the shipper, limits of liability exceeding those provided for in paragraph 1 may be fixed.

Article 7. Application to non-contractual claims

1. The defences and limits of liability provided for in this Convention apply in any action against the carrier in respect of loss of or damage to the goods covered by the contract of carriage by sea, as well as of delay in delivery whether the action is founded in contract, in tort or otherwise.
2. If such an action is brought against a servant or agent of the carrier, such servant or agent, if he proves that he acted within the scope of his employment, is entitled to avail himself of the defences and limits of liability which the carrier is entitled to invoke under this Convention.
3. Except as provided in article 8, the aggregate of the amounts recoverable from the carrier and from any persons referred to in paragraph 2 of this article shall not exceed the limits of liability provided for in this Convention.

Article 8. Loss of right to limit responsibility

1. The carrier is not entitled to the benefit of the limitation of liability provided for in article 6 if it is proved that the loss, damage or delay in delivery resulted from an act or omission of the carrier done with the intent to cause such loss, damage or delay, or recklessly and with knowledge that such loss, damage or delay would probably result.
2. Notwithstanding the provisions of paragraph 2 of article 7, a servant or agent of the carrier is not entitled to the benefit of the limitation of liability provided for in article 6 if it is proved that the loss, damage or delay in delivery resulted from an act or omission of such servant or agent, done with the intent to cause such loss, damage or delay, or recklessly and with knowledge that such loss, damage or delay would probably result.

Article 9. Deck cargo

1. The carrier is entitled to carry the goods on deck only if such carriage is in accordance with an agreement with the shipper or with the usage of the particular trade or is required by statutory rules or regulations.
2. If the carrier and the shipper have agreed that the goods shall or may be carried on deck, the carrier must insert in the bill of lading or other document evidencing the contract of carriage by sea a statement to that effect. In the absence of such a statement the carrier has the burden of proving that an agreement for carriage on deck has been entered into; however, the carrier is not entitled to invoke such an agreement against a third party, including a consignee, who has acquired the bill of lading in good faith.
3. Where the goods have been carried on deck contrary to the provisions of paragraph 1 of this article or where the carrier may not under paragraph 2 of this article invoke an agreement for carriage on deck, the carrier, notwithstanding the provisions of paragraph 1 of article 5, is liable for loss of or damage to the goods, as well as for delay in delivery, resulting solely from the carriage on deck, and the extent of his liability is to be determined in accordance with the provisions of article 6 or article 8 of this Convention, as the case may be.
4. Carriage of goods on deck contrary to express agreement for carriage under deck is deemed to be an act or omission of the carrier within the meaning of article 8.

Article 10. Liability of the carrier and actual carrier

1. Where the performance of the carriage or part thereof has been entrusted to an actual carrier, whether or not in pursuance of a liberty under the contract of carriage by sea to do so, the carrier nevertheless remains responsible for the entire carriage according to the provisions of this Convention. The carrier is responsible, in relation to the carriage performed by the actual carrier, for the acts and omissions of the actual carrier and of his servants and agents acting within the scope of their employment.
2. All the provisions of this Convention governing the responsibility of the carrier also apply to the responsibility of the actual carrier for the carriage performed by him. The provisions of paragraphs 2 and 3 of article 7 and of paragraph 2 of article 8 apply if an action is brought against a servant or agent of the actual carrier.

3. Any special agreement under which the carrier assumes obligations not imposed by this Convention or waives rights conferred by this Convention affects the actual carrier only if agreed to by him expressly and in writing. Whether or not the actual carrier has so agreed, the carrier nevertheless remains bound by the obligations or waivers resulting from such special agreement.
4. Where and to the extent that both the carrier and the actual carrier are liable, their liability is joint and several.
5. The aggregate of the amounts recoverable from the carrier, the actual carrier and their servants and agents shall not exceed the limits of liability provided for in this Convention.
6. Nothing in this article shall prejudice any right of recourse as between the carrier and the actual carrier.

Article 11. Through carriage

1. Notwithstanding the provisions of paragraph 1 of article 10, where a contract of carriage by sea provides explicitly that a specified part of the carriage covered by the said contract is to be performed by a named person other than the carrier, the contract may also provide that the carrier is not liable for loss, damage or delay in delivery caused by an occurrence which takes place while the goods are in the charge of the actual carrier during such part of the carriage. Nevertheless, any stipulation limiting or excluding such liability is without effect if no judicial proceedings can be instituted against the actual carrier in a court competent under paragraph 1 or 2 of article 21. The burden of proving that any loss, damage or delay in delivery has been caused by such an occurrence rests upon the carrier.
2. The actual carrier is responsible in accordance with the provisions of paragraph 2 of article 10 for loss, damage or delay in delivery caused by an occurrence which takes place while the goods are in his charge.

PART III. LIABILITY OF THE SHIPPERS

Article 12. General rule The shipper is not liable for loss sustained by the carrier or the actual carrier, or for damage sustained by the ship, unless such loss or damage was caused by the fault or neglect of the shipper, his servants or agents. Nor is any servant or agent of the shipper liable for such loss or damage unless the loss or damage was caused by fault or neglect on his part.

Article 13. Special rules on dangerous goods

1. The shipper must mark or label in a suitable manner dangerous goods as dangerous.
2. Where the shipper hands over dangerous goods to the carrier or an actual carrier, as the case may be, the shipper must inform him of the dangerous character of the goods and, if necessary, of the precautions to be taken. If the shipper fails to do so and such carrier or actual carrier does not otherwise have knowledge of their dangerous character:
   (a) the shipper is liable to the carrier and any actual carrier for the loss resulting from the shipment of such goods, and

(b) the goods may at any time be unloaded, destroyed or rendered innocuous, as the circumstances may require, without payment of compensation.

3. The provisions of paragraph 2 of this article may not be invoked by any person if during the carriage he has taken the goods in his charge with knowledge of their dangerous character.
4. If, in cases where the provisions of paragraph 2, subparagraph (b), of this article do not apply or may not be invoked, dangerous goods become an actual danger to life or property, they may be unloaded, destroyed or rendered innocuous, as the circumstances may require, without payment of compensation except where there is an obligation to contribute in general average or where the carrier is liable in accordance with the provisions of article 5.

PART IV. TRANSPORT DOCUMENTS

Article 14. Issue of bill of lading

1. When the carrier or the actual carrier takes the goods in his charge, the carrier must, on demand of the shipper, issue to the shipper a bill of lading.
2. The bill of lading may be signed by a person having authority from the carrier. A bill of lading signed by the master of the ship carrying the goods is deemed to have been signed on behalf of the carrier.
3. The signature on the bill of lading may be in handwriting, printed in facsimile, perforated, stamped, in symbols, or made by any other mechanical or electronic means, if not inconsistent with the law of the country where the bill of lading is issued.

Article 15. Contents of bill of lading

1. The bill of lading must include, inter alia, the following particulars:
   (a) the general nature of the goods, the leading marks necessary for identification of the goods, an express statement, if applicable, as to the dangerous character of the goods, the number of packages or pieces, and the weight of the goods or their quantity otherwise expressed, all such particulars as furnished by the shipper;
   (b) the apparent condition of the goods;
   (c) the name and principal place of business of the carrier;
   (d) the name of the shipper;
   (e) the consignee if named by the shipper;
   (f) the port of loading under the contract of carriage by sea and the date on which the goods were taken over by the carrier at the port of loading;
   (g) the port of discharge under the contract of carriage by sea;
   (h) the number of originals of the bill of lading, if more than one;
   (i) the place of issuance of the bill of lading;
   (j) the signature of the carrier or a person acting on his behalf;
   (k) the freight to the extent payable by the consignee or other indication that freight is payable by him;
   (l) the statement referred to in paragraph 3 of article 23;
   (m) the statement, if applicable, that the goods shall or may be carried on deck;

(n) the date or the period of delivery of the goods at the port of discharge if expressly agreed upon between the parties; and
(o) any increased limit or limits of liability where agreed in accordance with paragraph 4 of article 6.

2. After the goods have been loaded on board, if the shipper so demands, the carrier must issue to the shipper a 'shipped' bill of lading which, in addition to the particulars required under paragraph 1 of this article, must state that the goods are on board a named ship or ships, and the date or dates of loading. If the carrier has previously issued to the shipper a bill of lading or other document of title with respect to any of such goods, on request of the carrier the shipper must surrender such document in exchange for a 'shipped' bill of lading. The carrier may amend any previously issued document in order to meet the shippers demand for a 'shipped' bill of lading if, as amended, such document includes all the information required to be contained in a 'shipped' bill of lading.
3. The absence in the bill of lading of one or more particulars referred to in this article does not affect the legal character of the document as a bill of lading provided that it nevertheless meets the requirements set out in paragraph 7 of article 1.

Article 16. Bills of lading: reservations and evidentiary effect

1. If the bill of lading contains particulars concerning the general nature, leading marks, number of packages of pieces, weight or quantity of the goods which the carrier or other person issuing the bill of lading on his behalf knows or has reasonable grounds to suspect do not accurately represent the goods actually taken over or, where a 'shipped' bill of lading is issued, loaded, or if he had no reasonable means of checking such particulars, the carrier or such other person must insert in the bill of lading a reservation specifying these inaccuracies, grounds of suspicion or the absence of reasonable means of checking.
2. If the carrier or other person issuing the bill of lading on his behalf fails to note on the bill of lading the apparent condition of the goods, he is deemed to have noted on the bill of lading that the goods were in apparent good condition.
3. Except for particulars in respect of which and to the extent to which a reservation permitted under paragraph 1 of this article has been entered:
   (a) the bill of lading is prima facie evidence of the taking over or, where a 'shipped' bill of lading is issued, loading, by the carrier of the goods as described in the bill of lading; and
   (b) proof to the contrary by the carrier is not admissible if the bill of lading has been transferred to a third party, including a consignee, who in good faith has acted in reliance on the description of the goods therein.
4. A bill of lading which does not, as provided in paragraph 1, subparagraph (k), of article 15, set forth the freight or otherwise indicate that freight is payable by the consignee or does not set forth demurrage incurred at the port of loading payable by the consignee, is prima facie evidence that no freight or such demurrage is payable by him. However, proof to the contrary by the carrier is not admissible when the bill of lading has been transferred to a third party, including a

consignee, who in good faith has acted in reliance on the absence in the bill of lading of any such indication.

Article 17. Guarantees by the shipper

1. The shipper is deemed to have guaranteed to the carrier the accuracy of particulars relating to the general nature of the goods, their marks, number, weight and quantity as furnished by him for insertion in the bill of lading. The shipper must indemnify the carrier against the loss resulting from inaccuracies in such particulars. The shipper remains liable even if the bill of lading has been transferred by him. The right of the carrier to such indemnity in no way limits his liability under the contract of carriage by sea to any person other than the shipper.
2. Any letter of guarantee or agreement by which the shipper undertakes to indemnify the carrier against loss resulting from the issuance of the bill of lading by the carrier, or by a person acting on his behalf, without entering a reservation relating to particulars furnished by the shipper for insertion in the bill of lading, or to the apparent condition of the goods, is void and of no effect as against any third party, including a consignee, to whom the bill of lading has been transferred.
3. Such a letter of guarantee or agreement is valid as against the shipper unless the carrier or the person acting on his behalf, by omitting the reservation referred to in paragraph 2 of this article, intends to defraud a third party, including a consignee, who acts in reliance on the description of the goods in the bill of lading. In the latter case, if the reservation omitted relates to particulars furnished by the shipper for insertion in the bill of lading, the carrier has no right of indemnity from the shipper pursuant to paragraph 1 of this article.
4. In the case of intended fraud referred to in paragraph 3 of this article, the carrier is liable, without the benefit of the limitation of liability provided for in this Convention, for the loss incurred by a third party, including a consignee, because he has acted in reliance on the description of the goods in the bill of lading.

Article 18. Documents other than bills of lading Where a carrier issues a document other than a bill of lading to evidence the receipt of the goods to be carried, such a document is prima facie evidence of the conclusion of the contract of carriage by sea and the taking over by the carrier of the goods as therein described.

PART V. CLAIMS AND ACTIONS

Article 19. Notice of loss, damage or delay

1. Unless notice of loss or damage, specifying the general nature of such loss or damage, is given in writing by the consignee to the carrier not later than the working day after the day when the goods were handed over to the consignee, such handing over is prima facie evidence of the delivery by the carrier of the goods as described in the document of transport or, if no such document has been issued, in good condition.
2. Where the loss or damage is not apparent, the provisions of paragraph 1 of this article apply correspondingly if notice in writing is not given within 15 consecutive days after the day when the goods were handed over to the consignee.

3. If the state of the goods at the time they were handed over to the consignee has been the subject of a joint survey or inspection by the parties, notice in writing need not be given of loss or damage ascertained during such survey or inspection.
4. In the case of any actual or apprehended loss or damage, the carrier and the consignee must give all reasonable facilities to each other for inspecting and tallying the goods.
5. No compensation shall be payable for loss resulting from delay in delivery unless a notice has been given in writing to the carrier within 60 consecutive days after the day when the goods were handed over to the consignee.
6. If the goods have been delivered by an actual carrier, any notice given under this article to him shall have the same effect as if it had been given to the carrier; and any notice given to the carrier shall have effect as if given to such actual carrier.
7. Unless notice of loss or damage, specifying the general nature of the loss or damage, is given in writing by the carrier or actual carrier to the shipper not later than 90 consecutive days after the occurrence of such loss or damage or after the delivery of the goods in accordance with paragraph 2 of article 4, whichever is later, the failure to give such notice is prima facie evidence that the carrier or the actual carrier has sustained no loss or damage due to the fault or neglect of the shipper, his servants or agents.
8. For the purpose of this article, notice given to a person acting on the carriers or the actual carrier's behalf, including the master or the officer in charge of the ship, or to a person acting on the shipper's behalf is deemed to have been given to the carrier, to the actual carrier or to the shipper, respectively.

Article 20. Limitation of actions

1. Any action relating to carriage of goods under this Convention is time-barred if judicial or arbitral proceedings have not been instituted within a period of two years.
2. The limitation period commences on the day on which the carrier has delivered the goods or part thereof or, in cases where no goods have been delivered, on the last day on which the goods should have been delivered.
3. The day on which the limitation period commences is not included in the period.
4. The person against whom a claim is made may at any time during the running of the limitation period extend that period by a declaration in writing to the claimant. This period may be further extended by another declaration or declarations.
5. An action for indemnity by a person held liable may be instituted even after the expiration of the limitation period provided for in the preceding paragraphs if instituted within the time allowed by the law of the State where proceedings are instituted. However, the time allowed shall not be less than 90 days commencing from the day when the person instituting such action for indemnity has settled the claim or has been served with process in the action against himself.

Article 21. Jurisdiction

1. In judicial proceedings relating to carriage of goods under this Convention the plaintiff, at his option, may institute an action in a court which according to the

law of the State where the court is situated, is competent and within the jurisdiction of which is situated one of the following places:

(a) the principal place of business or, in the absence thereof, the habitual residence of the defendant; or
(b) the place where the contract was made, provided that the defendant has there a place of business, branch or agency through which the contract was made; or
(c) the port of loading or the port of discharge; or
(d) any additional place designated for that purpose in the contract of carriage by sea.

2. (a) Notwithstanding the preceding provisions of this article, an action may be instituted in the courts of any port or place in a Contracting State at which the carrying vessel or any other vessel of the same ownership may have been arrested in accordance with applicable rules of the law of that State and of international law. However, in such a case, at the petition of the defendant, the claimant must remove the action, at his choice, to one of the jurisdictions referred to in paragraph 1 of this article for the determination of the claim, but before such removal the defendant must furnish security sufficient to ensure payment of any judgement that may subsequently be awarded to the claimant in the action.
(b) All questions relating to the sufficiency or otherwise of the security shall be determined by the court of the port or place of the arrest.
3. No judicial proceedings relating to carriage of goods under this Convention may be instituted in a place not specified in paragraph 1 or 2 of this article. The provisions of this paragraph do not constitute an obstacle to the jurisdiction of the Contracting States for provisional or protective measures.
4. (a) Where an action has been instituted in a court competent under paragraphs 1 or 2 of this article or where judgement has been delivered by such a court, no new action may be started between the same parties on the same grounds unless the judgement of the court before which the first action was instituted is not enforceable in the country in which the new proceedings are instituted;
(b) For the purpose of this article, the institution of measures with a view to obtaining enforcement of a judgement is not to be considered as the starting of a new action;
(c) For the purpose of this article, the removal of an action to a different court within the same country, or to a court in another country, in accordance with paragraph 2 (a) of this article, is not to be considered as the starting of a new action.
5. Notwithstanding the provisions of the preceding paragraphs, an agreement made by the parties, after a claim under the contract of carriage by sea has arisen, which designates the place where the claimant may institute an action, is effective.

Article 22. Arbitration

1. Subject to the provisions of this article, parties may provide by agreement evidenced in writing that any dispute that may arise relating to carriage of goods under this Convention shall be referred to arbitration.

2. Where a charter-party contains a provision that disputes arising thereunder shall be referred to arbitration and a bill of lading issued pursuant to the charter-party does not contain special annotation providing that such provision shall be binding upon the holder of the bill of lading, the carrier may not invoke such provision as against a holder having acquired the bill of lading in good faith.
3. The arbitration proceedings shall, at the option of the claimant, be instituted at one of the following places:
   (a) a place in a State within whose territory is situated:
      (i) the principal place of business of the defendant or, in the absence thereof, the habitual residence of the defendant; or
      (ii) the place where the contract was made, provided that the defendant has there a place of business, branch or agency through which the contract was made; or
      (iii) the port of loading or the port of discharge; or
   (b) any place designated for that purpose in the arbitration clause or agreement.
4. The arbitrator or arbitration tribunal shall apply the rules of this Convention.
5. The provisions of paragraphs 2 and 4 of this article are deemed to be part of every arbitration clause or agreement, and any term of such clause or agreement which is inconsistent therewith is null and void.
6. Nothing in this article affects the validity of an agreement relating to arbitration made by the parties after the claim under the contract of carriage by sea has arisen.

PART VI. SUPPLEMENTARY PROVISIONS

Article 23. Contractual stipulations

1. Any stipulation in a contract of carriage by sea, in a bill of lading, or in any other document evidencing the contract of carriage by sea is null and void to the extent that it derogates, directly or indirectly, from the provisions of this Convention. The nullity of such a stipulation does not affect the validity of the other provisions of the contract or document of which it forms a part. A clause assigning benefit of insurance of goods in favour of the carrier, or any similar clause, is null and void.
2. Notwithstanding the provisions of paragraph 1 of this article, a carrier may increase his responsibilities and obligations under this Convention.
3. Where a bill of lading or any other document evidencing the contract of carriage by sea is issued, it must contain a statement that the carriage is subject to the provisions of this Convention which nullify any stipulation derogating therefrom to the detriment of the shipper or the consignee.
4. Where the claimant in respect of the goods has incurred loss as a result of a stipulation which is null and void by virtue of the present article, or as a result of the omission of the statement referred to in paragraph 3 of this article, the carrier must pay compensation to the extent required in order to give the claimant compensation in accordance with the provisions of this Convention for any loss of or damage to the goods as well as for delay in delivery. The carrier must, in addition, pay compensation for costs incurred by the claimant for the purpose of

exercising his right, provided that costs incurred in the action where the foregoing provision is invoked are to be determined in accordance with the law of the State where proceedings are instituted.

Article 24. General average

1. Nothing in this Convention shall prevent the application of provisions in the contract of carriage by sea or national law regarding the adjustment of general average.
2. With the exception of article 20, the provisions of this Convention relating to the liability of the carrier for loss of or damage to the goods also determine whether the consignee may refuse contribution in general average and the liability of the carrier to indemnify the consignee in respect of any such contribution made or any salvage paid.

Article 25. Other conventions

1. This Convention does not modify the rights or duties of the carrier, the actual carrier and their servants and agents provided for in international conventions or national law relating to the limitation of liability of owners of seagoing ships.
2. The provisions of articles 21 and 22 of this Convention do not prevent the application of the mandatory provisions of any other multilateral convention already in force at the date of this Convention relating to matters dealt with in the said articles, provided that the dispute arises exclusively between parties having their principal place of business in States members of such other convention. However, this paragraph does not affect the application of paragraph 4 of article 22 of this Convention.
3. No liability shall arise under the provisions of this Convention for damage caused by a nuclear incident if the operator of a nuclear installation is liable for such damage:
   (a) under either the Paris Convention of 29 July 1960 on Third Party Liability in the Field of Nuclear Energy as amended by the Additional Protocol of 28 January 1964, or the Vienna Convention of 21 May 1963 on Civil Liability for Nuclear Damage, or
   (b) by virtue of national law governing the liability for such damage, provided that such law is in all respects as favourable to persons who may suffer damage as is either the Paris Convention or the Vienna Convention.
4. No liability shall arise under the provisions of this Convention for any loss of or damage to or delay in delivery of luggage for which the carrier is responsible under any international convention or national law relating to the carriage of passengers and their luggage by sea.
5. Nothing contained in this Convention prevents a Contracting State from applying any other international convention which is already in force at the date of this Convention and which applies mandatorily to contracts of carriage of goods primarily by a mode of transport other than transport by sea. This provision

also applies to any subsequent revision or amendment of such international convention.

Article 26. Unit of account

1. The unit of account referred to in article 6 of this Convention is the special drawing right as defined by the International Monetary Fund. The amounts mentioned in article 6 are to be converted into the national currency of a State according to the value of such currency at the date of judgement or the date agreed upon by the parties. The value of a national currency, in terms of the special drawing right, of a Contracting State which a member of the International Monetary Fund is to be calculated in accordance with the method of valuation applied by the International Monetary Fund in effect at the date in question for its operations and transactions. The value of a national currency, in terms of the special drawing right, of a Contracting State which is not a member of the International Monetary Fund is to be calculated in a manner determined by that State.
2. Nevertheless, those States which are not members of the International Monetary Fund and whose law does not permit the application of the provisions of paragraph 1 of this article may, at the time of signature, or at the time of ratification, acceptance, approval or accession or at any time thereafter, declare that the limits of liability provided for in this Convention to be applied in their territories shall be fixed as 12,500 monetary units per package or other shipping unit or 37.5 monetary units per kilogram of gross weight of the goods.
3. The monetary unit referred to in paragraph 2 of this article corresponds to sixty-five and a half milligrams of gold of millesimal fineness nine hundred. The conversion of the amounts referred to in paragraph 2 into the national currency is to be made according to the law of the State concerned.
4. The calculation mentioned in the last sentence of paragraph 1 and the conversion mentioned in paragraph 3 of this article is to be made in such a manner as to express in the national currency of the Contracting State as far as possible the same real value for the amounts in article 6 as is expressed there in units of account. Contracting States must communicate to the depositary the manner of calculation pursuant to paragraph 1 of this article, or the result of the conversion mentioned in paragraph 3 of this article, as the case may be, at the time of signature or when depositing their instruments of ratification, acceptance, approval or accession, or when availing themselves of the option provided for in paragraph 2 of this article and whenever there is a change in the manner of such calculation or in the result of such conversion.

PART VII. FINAL CLAUSES

DELETED FOR THE PURPOSES OF THIS BOOK [deals with ratification, withdrawal by any Parties to it, variation of provisions, etc.]

Done at Hamburg, this thirty-first day of March one thousand nine hundred and seventy-eight, in a single original, of which the Arabic, Chinese, English, French, Russian and Spanish texts are equally authentic.

INDEX

For Product Safety Concerns and Information please contact our EU representative GPSR@taylorandfrancis.com
Taylor & Francis Verlag GmbH, Kaufingerstraße 24, 80331 München, Germany

www.ingramcontent.com/pod-product-compliance
Lightning Source LLC
LaVergne TN
LVHW082342011026
849160LV00025B/1590
9781032112862